The ABCs
of Socialism

EDITED BY
Bhaskar Sunkara

ILLUSTRATED BY
Phil Wrigglesworth

First published by Verso 2016
© Jacobin Foundation Ltd.

Verso
UK: 6 Meard Street, London W1F 0EG
US: 20 Jay Street, Suite 1010, Brooklyn, NY 11201

Verso is the imprint of New Left Books

ISBN-13: 978-1-78478-726-4

British Library Cataloguing in Publication Data
A catalog record for this book is available from the British
Library

Library of Congress Cataloging-in-Publication Data
A catalog record for this book is available from the Library
of Congress

Typeset in Antwerp by A2-Type
Printed in Canada

Among hundreds of others, this book was made possible by the generosity of:

Saki Bailey
Danny Bates
John Erganian
Marshall Mayer
David Mehan
Mark Ó Dochartaigh
Brian Skiffington
Frederick Sperounis
Francis Tseng
Nathan Zimmerman

Special thanks to the Anita L. Mishler Education Fund (nitafund@gmail.com)

This book contains in-text annotations for further reading. Some annotations contain <u>hyperlink</u> information for direct reference to articles in *Jacobin*'s online archive. Simply copy the digits included in the annotation to the end of the following URL for related articles:

www.jacobinmag.com/?p=<u>12345</u> ←·······

Article Title
Author • Jacobin • Date

<u>12345</u>

About the Authors

Nicole Aschoff is the managing editor at *Jacobin* and the author of *The New Prophets of Capital*.

Alyssa Battistoni is an editor at *Jacobin* and a PhD student in political science at Yale University.

Jonah Birch is a graduate student in sociology at New York University and a contributing editor at *Jacobin*.

Vivek Chibber is a professor of sociology at New York University. His latest book is *Postcolonial Theory and the Specter of Capital*.

Danny Katch is a contributor to *Socialist Worker* and the author of *Socialism … Seriously*.

Chris Maisano is a contributing editor at *Jacobin* and a union staffer in New York.

Nivedita Majumdar is an associate professor of English at John Jay College. She is the secretary of the Professional Staff Congress, the CUNY faculty and staff union.

Michael A. McCarthy is an assistant professor of sociology at Marquette University.

Joseph M. Schwartz is the national vice-chair of the Democratic Socialists of America and professor of political science at Temple University.

Bhaskar Sunkara is the founding editor and publisher of *Jacobin*.

Keeanga-Yamahtta Taylor is an assistant professor in Princeton University's Center for African American Studies and the author of *From #BlackLivesMatter to Black Liberation*.

Adaner Usmani is a graduate student at New York University and on the board of *New Politics*.

Erik Olin Wright is a professor of sociology at the University of Wisconsin–Madison. His latest book is *Alternatives to Capitalism: Proposals for a Democratic Economy*.

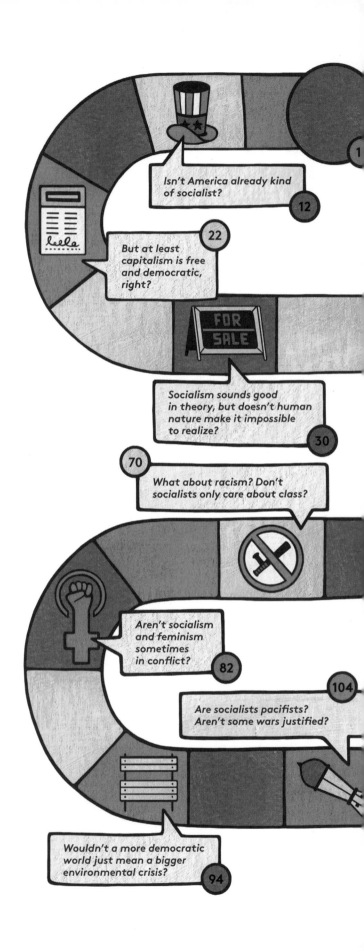

The ABCs of Socialism

The ABCs of Socialism was produced as a collaboration between Verso Books and *Jacobin* magazine, which is released online and quarterly in print to over 25,000 subscribers.

If you're interested in the ideas in this book, join a Jacobin reading group in over seventy cities across the world.

Visit www.jacobinmag.com/reading-groups/ for more details.

Contents

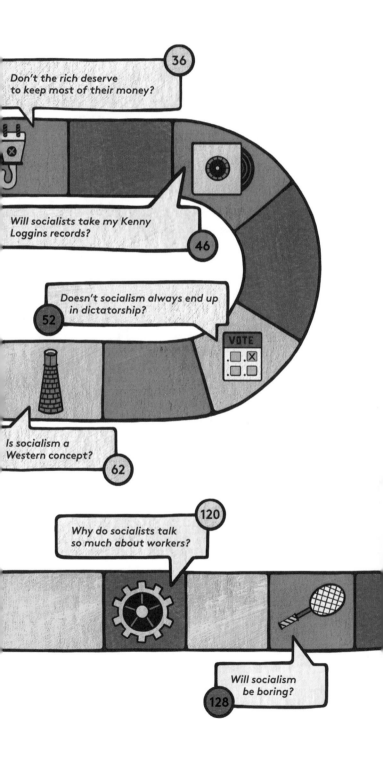

A little more than a century ago, socialism might not have been a mass force in American politics, but it seemed destined to become one.

In 1912, the Socialist Party won almost a million votes in the presidential election, had a membership of 120,000, and elected more than a thousand socialists to office. Mayors of cities like Berkeley, Flint, Milwaukee, and Schenectady were all socialists. So was a congressman, Victor Berger, and dozens of state officials.

That year, Oklahoma alone was home to eleven socialist weeklies. And in clusters of the country — from the Jewish enclaves of the Lower East Side to the mining towns of the West — the "cooperative commonwealth" was the dream to which all other political appeals were compared.

That commonwealth never came into being, and the decades that followed would be less kind to the Left. There were still upsurges and victories, of course, and socialists acquitted themselves well, helping build campaigns against oppression and exploitation. But as we entered the twenty-first century, socialism in the United States felt less like a live current and more like a dying piece of American history.

With the emergence of the Bernie Sanders campaign and new movements for democracy and freedom, this may be beginning to change. The events of this year all point to the emergence of "Sanders Democrats," a group that is disproportionately young and calling for massive redistributions of wealth and power. Sanders is only the beginning; this force will continue struggling for a different sort of politics.

Over the past six months, we've had more conversations about socialism with friends and strangers alike than in the last six years. *Jacobin's* subscriber rolls have increased by hundreds every week, and our inbox is flooded with emails asking basic definitional questions about socialism.

We don't have all the answers, but this book was made to help tackle some of them. The *ABCs of Socialism* will be useful for years to come — not only as a primer for future generations of radicals, but also as an artifact of a time when the socialist left was once again filled with promise. How this story ends is up to us.

Isn't America already kind of socialist?

Chris Maisano

If you spend much time on social media, you've probably seen the memes purporting to show just how socialist the United States already is by listing a bunch of government programs, services, and agencies. There are many variations on the theme, but my favorite one lists no less than fifty-five ostensibly socialist programs whose only commonality is that Uncle Sam carries them all out.

Some directly serve social needs and involve some measure of income redistribution (public libraries, welfare, the WIC program, Social Security, food stamps). Some seem thrown in for no good reason at all (Amber Alerts? The White House?). Others are basic operational activities that any modern government, regardless of its ideological orientation, would carry out (the census, fire departments, garbage and snow removal, sewers, street lighting). And still others involve the vast apparatus of coercion and force (police departments, the

So long as the fundamental structures of the economy remain unchanged, state action will disproportionately benefit capitalist interests at the expense of everything else.

FBI, the CIA, the military, courts, prisons, and jails).

For all of Bernie Sanders's virtues, his campaign for president has only thickened the fog of ideological confusion. At one campaign stop last year, he endorsed the thinking behind the most simplistic of these memes: "When you go to your public library, when you call your fire department or the police department, what do you think you're calling? These are socialist institutions." By that logic any sort of collective project funded by tax dollars and accomplished through government action is socialism.

It's not difficult to see the problem with this line of thinking. In a country as deeply and reflexively anti-statist as the United States, the identification of socialism with government is perhaps the worst possible rhetorical strategy the Left could adopt. "Like the DMV? Then You'll Love Socialism!" isn't a slogan that will win many converts. More importantly, conflating all government action with socialism forces us to defend many of the most <u>objectionable forms of state activity</u>, including

The Making of the American Police State
Christian Parenti • Jacobin • 7.28.2015

23608

those that we would want to abolish in a free and just society.

It's one thing to identify public libraries with socialism. They operate according to democratic principles of access and distribution, providing services to all regardless of one's ability to pay. They would be one of the most important institutions in any socialist society worthy of the name. But it's quite another to include the police. If the forces responsible for killing Sandra Bland, Eric Garner, and Rekia Boyd exemplify socialism in action, then no person who wants freedom and justice should be a socialist.

The idea that any government activity is synonymous with socialism has major political and strategic implications. After all, if our country were already at least partly socialist, then all we would have to do is keep gradually expanding government. We wouldn't have to change the purpose of any existing programs, nor would we have to reform the administrative structures of government agencies.

And because all of those purportedly socialist programs have been won without fundamentally challenging private property, there would be no need for a decisive confrontation with the owners of capital and their political allies. All we would have to do is elect sympathetic politicians to office and let them legislate their way to even more socialism.

Academics who study politics for a living often fall into this trap. By simply looking at the size of government in terms of overall spending, many argue that the US is becoming increasingly socialist whether it wants to or not. In their view major social reforms will happen willy-nilly, with a passive populace coming to support successful programs only after they have been legislated by politicians and implemented by bureaucrats.

Government spending on social programs and other activities may well increase in the coming decades because of the aging population, the climate crisis, and other developments. But the sheer volume of spending tells us little about the political valence of government action. Key questions about that state activity always need to be asked: does it reinforce or undermine the power of those who own capital? Does it increase our subordination to <u>market discipline</u> or offer us more freedom from its demands?

There have been a number of large-scale government initiatives since the 1980s, even during periods of Republican political dominance. But many of the biggest programs over the last few decades do nothing to strengthen the power of workers.

The Earned Income Tax Credit (EITC) has brought much-needed relief to the working poor, but it also serves as an indirect subsidy for low-wage employers. Medicare Part D offers some subsidies to low-income seniors, but it's widely recognized as a costly giveaway to the prescription drug industry.

Obamacare has increased health insurance coverage, partially through the (contested) expansion of Medicaid. But the individual mandate only serves to deepen marketization, adding millions of Americans to the private, for-profit insurance system. The 2009 stimulus plan likely saved the country from another Great Depression, but it was inadequate to the scale of the crisis and weighted in favor of

16716

Capitalism's Gravediggers • Ellen Meiksins Wood • Jacobin • 12.5.2014 tax cuts for businesses who simply pocketed the cash instead of hiring new workers. The list goes on.

Why does this happen? For one thing, the rich and powerful invest heavily in political activity to promote their interests and block progressive reforms. By the end of last year, the contributions of just 158 families and the companies they own (a staggering $176 million) made up about half the total funding in the 2016 presidential race. Through their political spending and the influence it buys, they have been able to shape tax and other policies for their own benefit, an advantage reinforced by favorable judicial decisions (e.g. *Citizens United*) and lobbying activities.

According to a widely noted 2014 study by two political scientists, the political dominance of the wealthy is now so pronounced that average citizens exercise "near zero" influence over government policymaking.

The middle and upper classes also hold the most important posts in government, elected and appointed alike. They share a common set of ideas and values predicated on protecting the status quo and repressing any major challenge to that system, particularly those that come from the working class and the Left.

These direct forms of influence are not the only way that powerful interests shape government action. After all, governments are dependent on some minimally robust level of economic activity to fund themselves. The tax revenues or debt financing governments rely on are directly related to the state of the capitalist economy and its rates of growth and profitability. If the level of economic activity declines — perhaps, because capitalists are unhappy about new legislation that benefits workers — the state will find it increasingly difficult to fund its activities. This in turn leads to a decline in its legitimacy and its level of popular support.

Because economic activity is significantly determined by the investment decisions of private capitalists, these forces can essentially <u>veto</u> government policies that they think are against their interests. Often, if capitalists aren't induced to make investments through business subsidies and other incentives, they simply will refuse to invest.

Consequently, there is a strong tendency for politicians and bureaucrats to align their policy decisions with the interests of capitalists in the private sector. Preserving "business confidence" is a major constraint on the formation of policy, and is one of the main reasons why government action is so often favorable to capitalist interests. It's also how they're able to conflate their own interests with a larger "public" or "national" interest — under a capitalist system, there's some truth to their claim.

In the absence of popular organization and militancy, government action will do little to shift the balance of power away from capital and toward labor, or to undermine market discipline instead of deepening it. So long as the fundamental structures of the economy remain unchanged, state action will disproportionately benefit capitalist interests at the expense of everything else.

This is not to say that progressive reforms can never be won under capitalism, or that the government is completely immune to public pressure. However, such reforms

In the absence of popular organization and militancy, government action will do little to shift the balance of power away from capital and toward labor.

have only been won with the support of direct, mass struggles against employers.

Simply electing politicians to office or watching the government expand by its own momentum has never been, and never will be, enough. Economic power is political power, and under capitalism the owners of capital will always have the capacity to undermine popular democracy — no matter who's in Congress or the White House.

Winning government power and using it to break the dominance of the capitalist class is a necessary condition for beginning the transition to socialism. A government run by a socialist party (or a coalition of left and working-class parties) would move to bring the economy's key industries and enterprises under some form of social control. But that alone wouldn't be sufficient. The bitter experiences of the twentieth century have taught us that socialism won't further the cause of human freedom if the political and administrative structures of government aren't thoroughly democratized.

Here is where continued popular mobilization outside (and, if necessary, against) formal political structures becomes absolutely crucial. In order to withstand the inevitable backlash from capitalist and conservative forces, a socialist transition would need to draw on mass popular support and direct participation in the affairs of government.

This would entail not only creating directly democratic bodies that supplant or complement representative institutions like Congress, but dramatically overhauling state agencies and administrative structures. Such an expansion of popular power would be needed to both push out personnel committed to the old regime and to transform the often alienating and repressive bureaucracies that currently administer public services.

Public schools, welfare departments, planning agencies, courts, and all other government agencies would invite workers and recipients to participate in the design and implementation of those services. Public-sector unions could play a key role in this endeavor, organizing both the providers and users of public services to radically transform the administrative structures of government.

Only under these conditions would government activity be synonymous with democratic socialism. Instead of posing an abstract concept of "government" against the forces of capital, we should begin the hard work of conceiving and building new institutions that can make government of the people, by the people, and for the people a reality. ■

No, socialism isn't just more government — it's about democratic ownership and control.

But at least capitalism is free and democratic, right?

Erik Olin Wright

In the United States, many take for granted that freedom and democracy are inextricably connected with capitalism. Milton Friedman, in his book *Capitalism and Freedom,* went so far as to argue that capitalism was a necessary condition for both.

It is certainly true that the <u>appearance</u> and spread of capitalism brought with it a tremendous expansion of individual freedoms and, eventually, popular struggles for more democratic forms of political organization. The claim that capitalism fundamentally obstructs both freedom and democracy will then sound strange to many.

To say that capitalism restricts the flourishing of these values is not to argue that capitalism has run counter to freedom and democracy in every instance. Rather, through the functioning of its most basic processes, capitalism generates severe deficits of both freedom and democracy that it can never remedy. Capitalism has promoted

The Origin of Capitalism: A Longer View
Ellen Meiksins Wood • Verso, 2002

the emergence of certain limited forms of freedom and democracy, but it imposes a low ceiling on their further realization.

At the core of these values is self-determination: the belief that people should be able to decide the conditions of their own lives to the fullest extent possible. When an action by a person affects only that person, then he or she ought to be able to engage in that activity without asking permission from anyone else. This is the context of freedom. But when an action affects the lives of others, then these other people should have a say in the activity. This is the context of democracy. In both, the paramount concern is that people retain as much control as possible over the shape their lives will take.

In practice, virtually every choice a person makes will have some effect on others. It is impossible for everyone to contribute to every decision that concerns them, and any social system that insisted on such comprehensive democratic participation would impose an unbearable burden on people. What we need, therefore, is a set of rules to distinguish between questions of freedom and those of democracy. In our society, such a distinction is usually made with reference to the boundary between the private and public spheres.

There is nothing natural or spontaneous about this line between the private and the public; it is forged and maintained by social processes. The tasks entailed by these processes are complex and often contested. The state vigorously enforces some public/private boundaries and leaves others to be upheld or dissolved as social norms. Often the boundary between the public and the private remains fuzzy. In a fully democratic society, the boundary itself is subject to democratic deliberation.

Capitalism constructs the boundary between the public and private spheres in a way that constrains the realization of true individual freedom and reduces the scope of meaningful democracy. There are five ways in which this is readily apparent.

1. "Work or Starve" Isn't Freedom

Capitalism is anchored in the private accumulation of wealth and the pursuit of income through the market. The economic inequalities that result from these "private" activities are intrinsic to capitalism and create inequalities in what the philosopher Philippe van Parijs calls "real freedom."

Whatever else we might mean by freedom, it must include the ability to say "no." A wealthy person can freely decide not to work for wages; a poor person without an independent means of livelihood cannot do so easily.

But the value of freedom goes deeper than this. It is also the ability to act positively on one's life plans — to choose not just an answer, but the question itself.

The children of wealthy parents can take unpaid internships to advance their careers; the children of poor parents cannot.

Capitalism deprives many people of real freedom in this sense. Poverty in the midst of plenty exists because of a direct equation between material resources and the resources needed for self-determination.

2. Capitalists Decide

The way the boundary between the public and private spheres is drawn in capitalism

In the Name of Love • Miya Tokumitsu • Jacobin • Issue 13

9534

excludes crucial decisions, which affect large numbers of people, from democratic control. Perhaps the most fundamental right that accompanies private owner-ship of capital is the right to decide to invest and disinvest strictly on the basis of self-interest.

A corporation's decision to move pro-duction from one place to another is a private matter, even though it makes a radical impact on the lives of everyone in both places. Even if one argues that this concentration of power in private hands is necessary for the efficient allocation of resources, the exclusion of these kinds of decisions from democratic control unequivocally decimates the capacity for self-determination by all except the owners of capital.

3. Nine to Five Is Tyranny

Capitalist firms are allowed to be organized as workplace dictatorships. An essential component of a business owner's power is the right to tell employees what to do. That is the basis of the employment contract: the job seeker agrees to follow the employer's orders in exchange for a wage.

Of course, an employer is also free to grant workers considerable autonomy, and in some situations this is the profit-maximizing way of organizing work. But such autonomy is given or withheld at the owner's pleasure. No robust conception of self-determination would allow autonomy to depend on the private preferences of elites.

A defender of capitalism might reply that a worker who doesn't like the boss's rule can always quit. But since workers by definition lack an independent means of livelihood, if they quit they will have to look for a new job and, to the extent that the available employment is in capitalist firms, they will still be subject to a boss's dictates.

4. Governments Have to Serve the Interests of Private Capitalists

Private control over major investment decisions creates a constant pressure on public authorities to enact rules favorable to the interests of capitalists. The threat of disinvestment and capital mobility is always in the background of public policy discussions, and thus politicians, whatever their ideological orientation, are forced to worry about sustaining a "good business climate."

Democratic values are hollow so long as one class of citizens takes priority over all others.

5. Elites Control the Political System

Finally, wealthy people have greater access than others to political power. This is the case in all capitalist democracies, although wealth-based inequality of political power is much greater in some countries than in others.

The specific mechanisms for this greater access are quite varied: contributions to political campaigns; financing lobbying efforts; elite social networks of various sorts; and outright bribes and other forms of corruption.

In the United States it is not only wealthy individuals, but also capitalist corporations, that face no meaningful restriction on their

Social Democracy's Incomplete Legacy • Chris Maisano • Jacobin • Issue 6

1221

ability to deploy private resources for political purposes. This differential access to political power voids the most basic principle of democracy.

• • •

These consequences are endemic to capitalism as an economic system. This does not mean that they cannot sometimes be mitigated in capitalist societies. In different times and places, many policies have been erected to compensate for capitalism's deformation of freedom and democracy.

Public constraints can be imposed on private investment in ways that erode the rigid boundary between the public and private; a strong public sector and active forms of state investment can weaken the threat of capital mobility; restrictions on the use of private wealth in elections and the public finance of political campaigns can reduce the privileged access of the wealthy to political power; labor law can strengthen the collective power of workers in both the political arena and the workplace; and a wide variety of welfare policies can increase the real freedom of those without access to private wealth.

When the political conditions are right, the anti-democratic and freedom-impeding features of capitalism can be palliated, but they cannot be eliminated. Taming capitalism in this way has been the central objective of the policies advocated by socialists within capitalist economies the world over.

But if freedom and democracy are to be fully realized, capitalism must not merely be tamed. It must be overcome.

It might seem that way, but genuine freedom and democracy aren't compatible with capitalism.

Socialism sounds good in theory, but doesn't human nature make it impossible to realize?

Adaner Usmani
& Bhaskar Sunkara

"Good in theory, bad in practice." People who profess interest in socialism and the idea of a society without exploitation and hierarchy are often met with this dismissive reply. Sure, the concept sounds nice, but people aren't very nice, right? Isn't capitalism much more suited to human nature — a nature dominated by competitiveness and venality?

Socialists don't believe these truisms. They don't view history as a mere chronicle of cruelty and selfishness. They also see countless acts of empathy, reciprocity, and love. People are complex: they do unspeakable things, but they also engage in remarkable acts of kindness and, even in difficult situations, show deep regard for others.

This does not mean that we're plastic — that there is no such thing as human nature. Progressives do sometimes make this claim, often arguing with those who see people as walking, talking utility-maximizers.

Despite its good intentions, this reproach goes too far.

For at least two reasons, socialists are committed to the view that all humans share some important interests. The first is a moral one. Socialists' indictment of how today's societies fail to provide necessities like food and shelter in a world of plenty, or stunt the development of people locked into thankless, grueling, low-paying jobs, rests on a core belief (stated or not) about the impulses and interests that animate people everywhere.

Our outrage that individuals are denied the right to live free and full lives is anchored in the idea that people are inherently creative and curious, and that capitalism too often stifles these qualities. Simply put, we strive for a freer and more fulfilling world because everyone, everywhere, cares about their freedom and fulfillment.

But this is not the only reason why socialists are interested in humanity's universal drives. Having a conception of human nature also helps us make sense of the world around us. And by helping us to interpret the world, it aids our efforts to change it, as well.

We strive for a freer and more fulfilling world because everyone, everywhere, cares about their freedom and fulfilment.

> *One of our principal tasks as socialists is to help make collective action a viable choice for even more people.*

Marx famously <u>said</u> that "the history of all hitherto existing society is the history of class struggles." Resistance to exploitation and oppression is a constant throughout history — it is as much a part of human nature as competitiveness, or greed. The world around us is filled with instances of people defending their lives and dignity. And while social structures may shape and constrain individual agency, there are no structures that steamroll people's rights and freedoms without inviting resistance.

Of course, the history of all "hitherto existing society" is also a record of passivity and even acquiescence. Mass collective action against exploitation and oppression is rare. If humans everywhere are committed to defending their individual interests, why don't we resist more?

Well, the view that all people have incentives to demand freedom and fulfillment does not imply that they will always have the capacity to do so. Changing the world is no easy feat. Under ordinary circumstances, the risks associated with acting collectively often seem overwhelming.

For example, workers who choose to join a union or go on strike to improve their working conditions may invite the scrutiny of their bosses and even lose their jobs.

12043

The Communist Manifesto
Karl Marx and Friedrich Engels • 1848

<u>Collective action</u> requires many different individuals to decide to take these risks together, so it's not surprising that it is uncommon and mostly fleeting.

Put differently, socialists don't believe that the absence of mass movements is a sign that people have no inherent desire to fight back, or worse, that they don't even recognize what their interests are. Rather, protest is uncommon because people are smart. They know that in the present political moment change is a risky, distant hope, so they develop other strategies to get by.

But sometimes people do step up and take risks. They organize and build progressive movements from below. History is filled with <u>examples</u> of people fighting against exploitation, and one of our principal tasks as socialists is to support these movements, to help make collective action a viable choice for even more people.

In this effort — and the struggle to define the values of a more just society — we will be aided, not hurt, by our shared nature. ∎

23500

Uniting the Dispossessed

Bryan D. Palmer • Jacobin • 7.22.2015

23847

The Second American Revolution

Bruce Levine • Jacobin • Issue 18

Our shared nature actually helps us build and define the values of a more just society.

Don't the rich deserve to keep most of their money?

Michael A. McCarthy

Tech tycoons, beloved entertainers, and dazzling athletes nearly always come up in heated debates over taxes. Don't you like your iPod? What about Harry Potter? Neoliberal economists argue that figures like Steve Jobs, J. K. Rowling, and LeBron James should make more money than the rest of us. After all, we — the consumers — are the ones buying their products. Their higher pay creates the incentive necessary for the hard work and innovation that even the lazy among us benefit from.

Intuitive as it may seem, this view doesn't hold up. Advocates for low taxes on the wealthy deliberately choose examples from tech and entertainment, suggesting that the elite are great innovators truly cut from a different cloth. But a glance at the list of the top paid CEOs in the United States tells us otherwise. The highest paid executive is Discovery Communications' David Zaslav, who made over $150 million in 2014. His great contribution to the

The socialist justification for taxes is grounded in a view — not often captured in opinion polls — about how capitalist wealth is actually created.

human endeavor? Helping to air "Here Comes Honey Boo Boo."

Most people understand this and believe the rich should pay more in taxes. According to a 2015 Gallup poll, 62 percent believe that upper-income earners are taxed "too little," while just 25 percent think they pay their "fair share." 69 percent believe corporations aren't taxed enough, while only 16 percent were content with current rates. But the socialist justification for taxes is grounded in a view — not often captured in opinion polls — about how capitalist wealth is actually created. To explore it, we first need to understand what taxes are and what non-socialists think about them.

Tax policy does two things in capitalist society. First, it determines what share of the total economic pie will be managed by the public, in the form of government revenue, and how much will be left to the use of private actors like individuals and corporations. Second, it stipulates how that public share is divvied up between the competing needs and wants of individuals, organizations, and corporations. The first is about resource control while the second is a matter of allocation.

Even when a government takes in high tax revenue, it does not necessarily put it to progressive ends. Just consider the huge benefits that flow to corporations through subsidies or <u>state-supported research and development</u>, and it's easy to see how governments can redistribute up, down, or horizontally. In a capitalist economy, where productive resources remain privately owned, socialists call for a significant portion of the social product to be controlled publicly and democratically redistributed downward.

However, in the United States today, the libertarian view that "taxation is theft" has seeped so deeply into everyday conceptions of property that even those who support progressive taxation often accept the premise that there is a pre-tax income that people earn and should own outright. Even the liberal credo that everyone needs to "do their fair share" is based on the implicit idea that workers and capital alike pay taxes out of a civic obligation to give up part of what is theirs for the betterment of society.

On the same grounds, libertarians argue that if pre-tax income is the direct product of a person or corporation's own effort, it should be theirs to use as they see fit. In this view, even if the government has decided democratically to tax the rich at a higher rate, taxation remains fundamentally unjust. In the extreme formulation of libertarian political philosopher Robert Nozick, "taxation of earnings from labor is on par with forced labor."

That viewpoint has been rightly criticized by progressives. But socialists should not fall back on the common liberal criterion for taxation: that a person or corporation's ability to pay should

20206

Red Innovation

Tony Smith • Jacobin • Issue 17

determine the amount they pay. The familiar justification circulates even among leftists, who hear within it an echo of the dictum "from each according to his abilities, to each according to his needs."

This perspective suggests one of two things, both of which are inaccurate. First, that taxes are a kind of necessary evil for those that are being taxed. Even though a person or corporation's pre-tax income is the result of their own labor, it's more practical for society to tax some of that income for public purposes than to leave it under private control. Or, alternatively, that taxing the rich more is just being fair. Both of these views get us tangled back in the <u>libertarian thicket</u> — doesn't such a tax policy still encroach on the rights of the individual? Should fairness then trump individual rights? And doesn't the socialist argument for heavy progressive taxation ultimately also violate the rights of the individual as well? Why do socialists hate freedom so much?

The socialist view of redistribution within a capitalist society must reject an important premise at play in nearly all tax policy debates: that pre-tax income is something earned solely by individual effort and possessed privately before the state intervenes to take a part of it. Once we break from this libertarian fantasy, it's easy to see that individual and corporate income is made possible only through tax-financed state action.

The capitalist economy is not self-regulating. The first precondition for firms to earn profits is state-enforced property rights, which give some people ownership and control over productive resources while excluding others. Second, governments

12084

The Limits of Libertarianism
Corey Robin • Jacobin • 7.12.2014

have to manage labor markets to help ensure that the skill needs of firms are met. States do this through setting immigration and education policies. All capitalist states also try to mitigate labor market risks, whether it be the risk of labor scarcity for firms or unemployment for workers. Third, most capitalists want states to enforce anti-trust, contract, criminal, property, and tort laws, as it makes market interactions more predictable and reliable. And finally, the capitalist economy needs a working infrastructure. Even most libertarians argue that state control over the money supply and interest rates is necessary to spur or slow growth when the economy needs it.

All of this is done with taxes. In short, the very notion of pre-tax income or profits is a bookkeeping trick. A person's income or a corporation's profits are in part the result of governments collecting taxes and actively creating the conditions under which they were able to make money in the first place. In this framework, "tax the rich" isn't merely a cry of spite or a demand for fairness.

The socialist case for taxation and progressive redistribution is built from three basic factors of how capitalism works. First, as just explored, personal incomes and corporate profits are not simply the result of individual work and business competition — instead they are part of a broader social product. The total income generated in a capitalist society is the result of a collective social effort, made possible by a specific social and legal architecture, and channeled through both publicly funded and privately controlled and financed institutions.

Second, the class inequality that results from making this social product is relational. Capitalists are able to accumulate large stores of wealth only because workers do not. All things being equal, firms can raise their profits in inverse proportion to the labor costs they bear. The condition for this relationship is, once again, political and maintained through tax revenue. Firms rely on states to enforce property rights and contracts that keep ownership of society's productive resources — its means of production — in the hands of very few. As a result, in capitalism, most people work for others; they don't hire others to work for them. And capitalists employ workers only when they believe that those workers' efforts are going to make the firm more money than they will take out in wages — doing otherwise would be market suicide.

Of course, hard work, guile, and luck afford some workers the ability to become capitalists. But the basic structure of capitalism, in which a small number own most of the productive assets, guarantees that the vast majority of people will (at best) spend their lives earning wages, but never profits. Taxation provides a partial remedy to that essential, structural inequality of capitalist society.

Third, <u>redistribution through taxation</u> is a means of extending individual freedom — not curtailing it, as libertarians contend. Freedom, according to the liberal theorist Isaiah Berlin, has a dual composition. On one side, there is negative freedom, the absence of coercion or "freedom from" that is the hallmark of most common conceptions of freedom in the United States today. With respect to coercion, taxes fund a variety of public provisions that offer citizens some measure of freedom from the private tyranny of firms. They form the

The Right to a Dignified Life • Jesse A. Myerson • Jacobin • 8.4.2015

23818

The very notion of pre-tax income or profits is a bookkeeping trick.

entire basis of the state apparatus that, in a capitalist system, is the only force whose power exceeds that of the capitalist class as a whole.

Without laws prohibiting slavery, written by legislatures and enforced in courts sustained by the public coffers, people would be compelled by threat of violence or starvation to work for no money at all. Without regulations, like those that demand at least minimal workplace safety or the ones that compel management to engage in collective bargaining, workers would lose what little say they have in how their work is organized.

In the context of tax policy, however, positive freedom matters as well. Positive freedom is the "ability to" — the capacity to do things, and the possibility of selecting goals and making efforts to realize them. Such freedom requires resources. In capitalist societies with low levels of redistribution, positive freedom is a zero-sum game in which a few enjoy a great deal of such abilities at the expense of many others. Tax policy that divides the social product in such a way that allows some people to live opulent lives while others scrape by cannot be said to promote freedom. The public education system, for example, which offers citizens the opportunity to develop knowledge and skills in pursuit of both collective

The Truth About Finance
Stephen Maher • Jacobin • 1.5.2016

27860

and individual ambitions, is a bedrock of positive freedom that can only be sustained through taxation.

In a truly socialist society, the combination of political and economic equality would offer everyone a far greater degree of both negative and positive freedom than they enjoy under capitalism. Until we realize that world, progressive redistribution through taxation is both a means to redress structural inequalities and the primary way we can expand and extend freedom to as many people as possible.

But we are headed down the wrong path. Over the past few decades, financial gains from growing labor productivity have primarily flowed to the top while tax rates on top earners have been drastically lowered and now approach pre–New Deal levels. Even a modest increase in the total tax burden on the top 1 percent of earners to a 45 percent rate, far lower than its postwar levels, would bring in an additional $275 billion in revenue. That's far more than just the $47 billion needed to make all public colleges and universities tuition free. Such increases also go a long way in generating the revenue needed to finance a <u>universal health care system</u>, increase Social Security benefits, and rebuild our crumbling infrastructure.

Most would agree that we all deserve to live in a society where we are given what we deserve, are free, and have the capacity to be creative and reach our potential. As unglamorous as it may seem, redistributive taxation is a step in this direction. The rich didn't earn their wealth — they're just holding on to it for us. ■

Wealth is socially created — redistribution just allows more people to enjoy the fruits of their labor.

Will socialists take my Kenny Loggins records?

Bhaskar Sunkara

John Lennon's iconic 1971 single "Imagine" asks listeners to envision a world without possessions, one without greed or hunger, in which the Earth's treasures are shared by all humanity. It's not surprising that the song became an anthem for generations of dreamers, but it also captures something about the socialist vision — the powerful desire to end misery and oppression, and help every person reach their fullest potential.

But the picture painted by Lennon's song might be a bit worrying for those of us who don't want a world without personal possessions — a sort of global commune where we're forced to wear hemp bracelets and share our Kenny Loggins records.

Thankfully, socialists are not interested in collectivizing your music. It's not because we don't love Loggins. We simply don't want a world without personal property — the things meant for individual consumption. Instead, socialists strive for a society without private property — the things that give the people who own them power over those who don't.

The power created by private property is expressed most clearly in the labor market, where business owners get to decide who deserves a job and who doesn't, and are able to impose working conditions that, if given a fair alternative, ordinary people would otherwise reject. And even though workers do most of the actual work at a job, owners have unilateral say over how profits are divided up and don't compensate employees for all the value they produce. Socialists call this phenomenon exploitation.

Exploitation is not unique to capitalism. It's around in any class society, and simply means that some people are compelled to labor under the direction of, and for the benefit of, others.

Compared to systems of slavery or serfdom, the hardships many workers face today are less immediately obvious. In most countries they have real legal protections and can afford basic necessities — a result of battles won by labor movements to limit the scope and intensity of exploitation.

But exploitation is only ever mitigated in capitalism, never eliminated. Consider this (admittedly abstract) example: let's say that you're getting paid $15 an hour by a business owner in a stable, profitable firm. You've been working there five years, and you put in about sixty hours a week.

No matter what your job is like — whether it's easy or grueling, boring or exciting — one thing is certain: your labor is making more (probably a lot more) than $15 an hour for your boss. That persistent difference between what you produce and

Radically changing things would mean taking away the source of capitalists' power: the private ownership of property.

what you get back in return is exploitation — a key source of profits and wealth in capitalism.

And, of course, with your paycheck you're forced to buy all the things necessary for a good life — housing, health care, childcare, a college education — which are also commodities, produced by other workers who are not fully remunerated for their efforts either.

Radically changing things would mean taking away the source of capitalists' power: the private ownership of property.

In a socialist society — even one in which <u>markets</u> are retained in spheres like consumer goods — you and your fellow workers wouldn't spend your day making others rich. You would keep much more of the value you produced. This could translate into more material comfort, or, alternatively, the possibility of deciding to work less with no loss in compensation so you could go to school or take up a hobby.

This might seem like a pipe dream, but it's entirely plausible. Workers at all levels of design, production, and delivery know how to make the things society needs — <u>they do it every day</u>. They can run their workplaces collectively, cutting out the

The Red and the Black
Seth Ackerman • Jacobin • Issue 9

5487

Chasing Utopia
Sam Gindin • Jacobin • 3.10.2016

29390

middle-men who own private property. Indeed, democratic control over our workplaces and the other institutions that shape our communities is the key to ending exploitation.

That's the socialist vision: abolishing private ownership of the things we all need and use — factories, banks, offices, natural resources, utilities, communication and transportation infrastructure — and replacing it with social ownership, thereby undercutting the power of elites to hoard wealth and power. And that's also the ethical appeal of socialism: a world where people don't try to control others for personal gain, but instead cooperate so that everyone can flourish.

As for personal property, you can keep your Kenny Loggins records.

In fact, in a society free from the destructive economic busts endemic to capitalism, with <u>more employment security</u>, and necessities removed from the sphere of the market, your record collection would be free from the danger zone because you wouldn't have to pawn it for rent money.

That's socialism in a nutshell: less John Lennon, more Kenny Loggins. ∎

Socialists want a world without private property, not personal property. You can keep your terrible music.

Doesn't socialism always end up in dictatorship?

Joseph M. Schwartz

A generation of Americans has been taught that the Cold War was one fought between freedom and tyranny, with the outcome decisively won in favor of democratic capitalism. Socialism, of all stripes, was conflated with the crimes of the Soviet Union and doomed to the trash heap of bad ideas.

Yet many socialists were consistent opponents of authoritarianism of both left and right varieties. Marx himself understood that only by the power of their democratic numbers could workers create a socialist society. To that end, *The Communist Manifesto* ends with a clarion call for workers to win the battle for democracy against aristocratic and reactionary forces.

Legions of socialists followed this path, ardently defending political and civil rights, while also fighting to democratize control over economic and cultural life through expanded social rights and workplace democracy. Despite the common assertion that "capitalism equals democracy," capitalists themselves, absent the pressure from an organized working class, have never supported democratic reforms. While universal suffrage for white men came to the United States by the Jacksonian period, European socialists had to fight until the end of the nineteenth century against authoritarian capitalist regimes in Germany, France, Italy, and elsewhere to achieve the vote for working-class and poor men. Socialists gained popular support as the most consistent supporters of universal male suffrage — and eventually, women's suffrage — as well as the legal right to form unions and other voluntary associations.

Socialists and their allies in the labor movement have also long understood that people in a dire state of need cannot be free people. Thus, the socialist tradition is popularly identified outside the United States with winning the public provision of education, health care, child care, and old-age pensions and within the United States for backing many of these struggles.

For many socialists, the support for democratic reforms was unconditional; but they also believed that the class power needed

While criticizing capitalism as anti-democratic, democratic socialists have consistently opposed authoritarian governments that claim to be socialist.

to restrain the power of capital had to be furthered so that working people could fully control their social and economic destiny. While criticizing capitalism as anti-democratic, democratic socialists consistently opposed authoritarian governments that claim to be socialist.

Revolutionaries such as Rosa Luxemburg and Victor Serge criticized early Soviet rule for banning opposition parties, eliminating experiments in workplace democracy, and failing to embrace political pluralism and civil liberties. If the state owns the means of production, the question remains: how democratic is the state? As Luxemburg wrote in her 1918 pamphlet on the Russian Revolution:

> Without general elections, without freedom of the press, freedom of speech, freedom of assembly, without the free battle of opinions, life in every public institution withers away, becomes a caricature of itself, and bureaucracy rises as the only deciding factor.

Luxemburg understood that the 1871 Paris Commune, the brief experiment in radical democracy that Marx and Engels referred to as a true working-class government, had multiple political parties in its municipal council, only one of which was affiliated with Marx's International Workingmen's Association. True to these values, socialists, dissident communists, and independent trade unionists led the democratic rebellions against Communist rule in East Germany in 1953, Hungary in 1956, and Poland in 1956, 1968, and 1980. Democratic socialists also led the brief, but extraordinary experiment of "socialism with a human face" under the

The Russian Revolution
Rosa Luxemburg • 1918

The Civil War in France
Karl Marx • 1871

Dubček government in Czechoslovakia in 1968. All these rebellions were crushed by Soviet tanks.

The Soviet Union's fall, however, hardly meant that democracy was won. Socialists reject the claim that capitalist democracy is fully democratic. In fact, the affluent have abandoned their commitment to even basic democracy when they felt threatened by worker movements.

Marx's analysis in *The Eighteenth Brumaire* of French capitalist support for Louis Napoleon's coup against the French Second Republic chillingly prefigures capital's later support of fascism in the 1930s. In both cases, a declining petty bourgeoisie, a besieged middle class, and traditional agrarian elites gained the support of capitalists to thwart rising working-class militancy by overthrowing democratic governments. The authoritarian regimes of the 1970s and 1980s in Latin America likewise drew on corporate support of a similar nature. Much of the prestige of the postwar European left and today's Latin American left stemmed from their being the most consistent opponents of fascism.

The socialist and the anticolonial movements of the twentieth century understood that the revolutionary democratic goals of equality, liberty, and fraternity could not be realized if unequal economic power can be transformed into political power and if workers are dominated by capital. Socialists fight for economic democracy out of the radical democratic belief that "what touches all should be decided by all."

The capitalist argument that individual choice in the market equals freedom masks the reality that capitalism is an undemocratic system in which most people spend much of their life being "bossed." Corporations are forms of hierarchical dictatorships, as those who work in them have no voice in how they produce, what they produce, and how the profit they create is utilized. Radical democrats believe that binding authority (not just the law, but also the power to determine the division of labor in a firm) is only valid if every member of the institution affected by its practices has an equal voice in the making of those decisions.

Democratizing a complex economy would likely take a variety of institutional forms, ranging from worker ownership and cooperatives, to state ownership of financial institutions and natural monopolies (such as telecommunications and energy) — as well as international regulation of labor and environmental standards.

The overall structure of the economy would be determined through democratic politics and not by state bureaucrats. But the question remains: how to move beyond capitalist oligarchy to socialist democracy? By the late 1970s, many democratic socialists recognized that corporate profitability had been squeezed by the constraints the labor, feminist, environmental, and anti-racist movements of the 1960s placed on capital. They understood that capitalists would retaliate through political mobilization, outsourcing, and capital strikes. Thus, across Europe, socialists pushed for reforms aimed at winning greater public control over investment. The Swedish labor movement embraced the Meidner Plan, a program which would have taxed corporate profits over a twenty-five-year period to create public ownership of major firms. A Socialist-Communist coalition that elected

The Great Reformer
Kjell Östberg • Jacobin • 9.10.2015

24895

François Mitterrand to the French presidency in 1981 nationalized 30 percent of French industry and radically enhanced collective bargaining rights.

In response, French and Swedish capital invested abroad instead of at home, creating a recession that halted these promising moves toward democratic socialism. The policies of Thatcher and Reagan, which ushered in over thirty years of de-unionization and cuts to the safety net, confirmed the Left's prediction that either socialists would move beyond the welfare state to democratic control over capital or capitalist power would erode the gains of postwar social democracy.

Today, socialists across the world face the daunting challenge of how to rebuild working-class political power strong enough to defeat the consensus of both conservatives and Third Way social democrats in favor of corporate-dictated austerity.

But what of the many governments in the developing world that still call themselves socialist, particularly one-party states? In many ways, one-party Communist states shared more in common with past authoritarian capitalist "developmentalist" states — such as late nineteenth-century Prussia and Japan, and postwar South Korea and Taiwan — than with the vision of democratic socialism. These governments prioritized state-led industrialization over democratic rights, particularly those of an independent labor movement.

Neither Marx nor classic European socialism anticipated that revolutionary socialist parties might most readily seize power in predominantly agrarian, autocratic societies. In part, these parties were based in a nascent working class radicalized

Socialists fight for economic democracy out of the radical belief that "what touches all should be decided by all."

by the exploitation of foreign capital. But in China and Russia, the Communists also came to power because the aristocracy and warlords failed to defend the people against invasion — defeated peasant armies wanted peace and land. The Marxist tradition had little to say about how predominantly agrarian and postcolonial societies could develop in an equitable and democratic manner. What history does tell us is that trying to force peasants who had just been given private land by Communist revolutionaries back onto collective state farms results in brutal civil wars that sets back economic development for decades.

Contemporary economic reforms in China, Vietnam, and Cuba favor a mixed-market economy with a significant role for foreign capital and private land-owning peasants. But one-party elites instituting these experiments in economic pluralism have almost always repressed advocates of political pluralism, civil liberties, and labor rights. Despite continuous state harassment, the growing independent labor struggles in places like China and Vietnam may revive the working class's role in promoting democracy. It is in those movements, not in autocratic governments, that socialists place their solidarity.

China in Revolt • Eli Friedman • Jacobin • Issue 7/8

3715

Of course, there also exists a rich history of experiments in democratic socialism in the developing world, ranging from the 1970s Popular Unity government of Salvador Allende in Chile to the early years of Michael Manley's government in Jamaica that same decade. The Latin American "pink tide" in Bolivia, Venezuela, Ecuador, and Brazil today represents diverse experiments in democratic development — though their governing policies depend more on redistributing earnings from commodity exports than on restructuring economic power relations. But the United States government and global capitalist interests consistently work to undermine even these modest efforts at economic democracy.

The CIA and British intelligence overthrew the democratically-elected Mohammad Mosaddegh government in Iran in 1954 when it nationalized British oil. The International Monetary Fund and World Bank cut off credit to Chile and the CIA actively aided Augusto Pinochet's brutal military coup in that country. The United States likewise colluded with the IMF to squeeze the Manley-era Jamaican economy.

Capitalist hostility to even moderate reformist governments in the developing world knows no bounds. The US forcibly overthrew both the Jacobo Árbenz government in Guatemala in 1954 and the Juan Bosch presidency in the Dominican Republic in 1965 because they favored modest land reform. For students of history, the question should be not whether socialism necessarily leads to dictatorship, but whether a revived socialist movement can overcome the oligarchic and anti-democratic nature of capitalism. ■

Socialism is often conflated with authoritarianism. But historically, socialists have been among democracy's staunchest advocates.

Is socialism a Western concept?

Nivedita Majumdar

Socialism is in the air. It returned to the United States with the 2008 economic crisis, which made capitalism's exploitative nature clear for a new generation, and unleashed struggles to challenge austerity and staggering income inequality. Activists in a host of movements helped create the environment in which a presidential candidate could talk about socialism on a national stage.

Though he might not be the most radical of figures, Bernie Sanders, who openly identifies as a socialist, is drawing tens of thousands to his campaign, upending everyone's expectations.

It's no surprise, then, that the idea of socialism also faces heavy counterattack — and not only from the Right. Within the Left itself, there is suspicion of an ideal many view as single-mindedly focused on economic issues and distant from other everyday sufferings, especially those of black and brown people. Sanders's specific evocation of Scandinavian social democracy has elicited criticisms that he endorses a kind of "Nordic exceptionalism" that is hostile to diversity. Such attacks on even the tamest varieties of socialism are nourished, especially on college campuses, by theoretical positions that see Marxism and many of its descendants as <u>hopelessly Eurocentric</u>.

The underlying assumption in these related lines of attack is that socialism, a supposedly Western (and white) ideology, while capable of addressing economic injustices, remains incapable of speaking to the lived experience of oppression and discrimination in the Global South, as well as oppressed groups elsewhere.

Is there any validity in this criticism? The socialist ideal rests on the belief that working people all over the world suffer at the hands of capitalists and share a common interest in resisting exploitation. To call that a narrowly Western idea would be news to the more than 1,100 garment workers in Dhaka, Bangladesh, who were killed in April 2013 when the Rana Plaza factory building in which they were working <u>collapsed on them</u>. The building had been declared a safety hazard, but their employers forced them in under threat of dismissal.

Two years after the factory's collapse, Human Rights Watch conducted a detailed study of industry practices in Bangladesh. It found severe industry-wide retaliation against labor organizing, which is the one effective safeguard against hazardous work conditions and dismal wages. In order to stop union activities, factory owners routinely led vicious campaigns of intimidation and retaliation against workers, most of them women. Workers attempting to

7014

How Does the Subaltern Speak?
Vivek Chibber • Jacobin • Issue 10

11608

After Rana Plaza
Colin Long • Jacobin • 6.6.2014

spearhead organizing drives not only lost their jobs, but were often blacklisted across the sector.

On the other side of the globe, in April 2015, Walmart closed five of its American stores, laying off 2,200 workers with only a few hours' notice. While the stated reason for the closures was "plumbing repairs," it was a retaliatory action against workers trying to organize for a living wage and better work conditions. Walmart, where workers recently went on hunger strike to protest poverty wages, is the United States' largest employer of blacks, Hispanics, and women.

Is it Eurocentric to argue that Bangladeshi garment workers have as much at stake in fighting for their economic rights — for a decent livelihood and job security — as workers laid off at American Walmart stores? Certainly their Bangladeshi managers and factory owners don't think so. They are no less worried about, and no less hostile to, the idea of workers organizing than are the managers of Walmart.

Capitalists everywhere see workers as a source of profit. In a system driven solely by the profit motive, there is little incentive to address workers' needs beyond the dictates of the market. And the laws of the market, whatever the claims of neoclassical economics, are not fair or impartial. The superior economic and political might of capital ensures that the market's laws are always fixed in its favor.

In both contexts, however, a socialist analysis points to another reality at work. Against all odds, workers invariably fight back. But it's always an agonizing battle, with capital using every weapon in its arsenal to crush workers' resistance. The bosses' crude methods include physical intimidation when they can get away with it, as in Bangladesh, and more polished gambits, like closing down entire stores, as in the United States. For labor, the result of the battle is always risky and unpredictable because capital retaliates against dissent at every step. But capital can never be fully at ease, either, because exploitation everywhere breeds resistance.

Socialism is not Eurocentric because the logic of capital is universal — and so is <u>resistance against it</u>. Cultural specificities may shape some details of capital's operation differently in the United States and in Bangladesh, in France and in Nicaragua, but they do not alter its fundamental prioritization of profits over people. This is why, for more than a hundred years, many of the most powerful and sweeping social movements in the Global South have been inspired by the socialist ideal.

Whatever their differences, leaders as diverse as Mao Zedong in China, Kwame Nkrumah in Ghana, Walter Rodney in Guyana, Chris Hani in South Africa, Amílcar Cabral in Guinea-Bissau, M. N. Roy in India, and Che Guevara across Latin America saw socialism as a theory and practice no less relevant to their experience than it was for European trade unionists. And yes, these revolutionaries also faced political opponents who dismissed their cause as a theory of the West, unsuited to Eastern realities: the leaders of the religious right, landed classes, and other economic elites.

On the fateful morning of the Rana Plaza collapse, workers were reluctant to go into the building. Large cracks had appeared on the walls of the factory and inspectors had declared the building a hazard. But management forced them to start working. A devastated mother later recalled that her eighteen-year-old daughter, who perished in the collapse, had been threatened with loss of pay for the entire month if she chose not to work that day. This is a specific kind

11866

Why We're Marxists
Nivedita Majumdar • Jacobin • 7.2.2014

"The crime of capitalism is that it forces the vast majority of the population to remain preoccupied with basic concerns of nutrition, housing, health, and skill acquisition. It leaves little time for fostering the community and creativity that humans crave."

of dehumanization, born of deprivation and powerlessness and familiar to workers in every part of the world, who are forced to choose between their livelihood and their safety. Socialism identifies the source of such dehumanization — private ownership and exploitation — and rejects it.

Capitalism does not merely oppress workers on the factory floor. It creates an entire culture in which the logic of oppression and competition become common sense. It turns people against each other and their own humanity. Like Franz Kafka's character in *The Metamorphosis*, Gregor Samsa, people are alienated from their human selves, isolated from their fellow beings, and tortured by the loss of all that could be possible.

There is nothing Eurocentric in rejecting the destructive logic of capital and fighting for a better world to replace it. It is the genuinely universal and humane choice. ∎

Socialism is not Eurocentric because the logic of capital is universal — and so is resistance against it.

What about racism?
Don't socialists
only care about class?

Keeanga-Yamahtta Taylor

The Poverty of Culture
Jonah Birch & Paul Heideman • Jacobin • 9.6.2014

13783

For more than a year, the "Black Lives Matter" movement has gripped the United States. The movement's central slogan is a simple, declarative recognition of black humanity in a society that is wracked by economic and social inequality that are disproportionately experienced by African Americans.

The movement is relatively new, but the racism that spawned it is not. By every barometer in American society — health care, education, employment, poverty — African Americans are worse off. Elected officials from across the political spectrum often blame these disparities on an absence of "personal responsibility" or view them as a cultural phenomenon particular to African Americans.

In reality, racial inequality has been largely produced by government policy and private institutions that not only impoverish African Americans but also demonize and criminalize them.

Winning ordinary whites to an antiracist program is a key component in building a genuine, unified mass movement capable of challenging capital.

Yet racism is not simply a product of errant public policy or even the individual attitudes of racist white people — and understanding the roots of racism in American society is critical for eradicating it. Crafting better public policy and banning discriminatory behavior by individuals or institutions won't do the job. And while there is a serious need for government action banning practices that harm entire groups of people, these strategies fail to grasp the scale and depth of racial inequality in the United States.

To understand why the United States seems so resistant to racial equality, we have to look beyond the actions of elected officials or even those who prosper from racial discrimination in the private sector. We have to look at the way American society is organized under capitalism.

Divide and Rule

Capitalism is an economic system based on the exploitation of the many by the few. Because of the gross inequality it produces, capitalism relies on various political, social, and ideological tools to rationalize that inequality while simultaneously dividing the majority, who have every interest in uniting to resist it.

How does the 1 percent maintain its disproportionate control of the wealth and resources in American society? By a process of divide and rule.

Racism is only one among many oppressions intended to serve this purpose. For example, American racism developed under the regime of slavery as a justification for the enslavement of Africans at a time when the world was celebrating the concepts of liberty, freedom, and self-determination.

The dehumanization and subjection of black people had to be rationalized in this moment of new political possibilities. But the central objective was preserving the institution of slavery and the enormous riches that it produced.

As Karl Marx recognized:

> Direct slavery is just as much the pivot of bourgeois industry as machinery, credits, etc. Without slavery you have no cotton; without cotton you have no modern industry. It is slavery that has given the colonies their value; it is the colonies that have created world trade, and it is world trade that is the pre-condition of large-scale industry. Thus slavery is an economic category of the greatest importance.

Marx also identified the centrality of African slave labor to the genesis of capitalism when he wrote that "the discovery of gold and silver in America, the extirpation, enslavement and entombment in mines of the aboriginal population, the beginning of the conquest and looting of the East Indies, the turning of Africa into a warren for the commercial hunting of Black skins, signalized the rosy dawn of the era of capitalist production."

The labor needs of capital alone could explain how racism functioned under capitalism. The <u>literal dehumanization</u> of Africans for the sake of labor was used to justify their harsh treatment and their debased status in the United States.

This dehumanization did not simply end when slavery was abolished; instead, the mark of inferiority branded onto black skin carried over into Emancipation and laid the basis for the second-class citizenship African Americans experienced for close to a hundred years after slavery.

The debasement of blacks also made African Americans more vulnerable to economic coercion and manipulation — not just "anti-blackness." Coercion and manipulation were rooted in the evolving economic demands of capital, but their impact rippled far beyond the economic realm. Black people were stripped of their right to vote, subjected to wanton violence, and locked into menial and poorly paid labor. This was the political economy of American racism.

There was another consequence of racism and the marking of blacks. African Americans were so thoroughly banished from political, civil, and social life that it was virtually impossible for the vast majority of poor and working-class whites to even conceive of uniting with blacks to challenge the rule and authority of the ruling white clique.

Marx recognized this basic division within the working class when he observed, "In the United States of America, every independent movement of the workers was paralyzed as long as slavery

22959

How Race is Conjured • Jacobin • 6.29.2015

Barbara J. Fields & Karen E. Fields

disfigured a part of the Republic. Labor cannot emancipate itself in the white skin where in the black it is branded."

Marx grasped the modern dynamics of racism as the means by which workers who had common objective interests could also become mortal enemies because of subjective — but nevertheless real — racist and nationalist ideas. Looking at the tensions between Irish and English workers, Marx wrote:

> Every industrial and commercial center in England possesses a working class divided into two hostile camps, English proletarians and Irish proletarians. The ordinary English worker hates the Irish worker as a competitor who lowers his standard of life. In relation to the Irish worker he feels himself a member of the ruling nation and so turns himself into a tool of the aristocrats and capitalists of his country against Ireland …
>
> This antagonism is artificially kept alive and intensified by the press, the pulpit, the comic papers, in short by all the means at the disposal of the ruling classes. This antagonism is the secret of the impotence of the English working class, despite its organization. It is the secret by which the capitalist maintains its power. And that class is fully aware of it.

For socialists in the United States, recognizing the centrality of racism in dividing the class that has the actual power to undo capitalism has typically meant that socialists have been heavily involved in campaigns and social movements to end racism.

But within the socialist tradition, many have also argued that because African Americans and most other nonwhites are disproportionately poor and working class, campaigns aimed at ending economic inequality alone would stop their oppression.

This stance ignores how racism constitutes its own basis for oppression for nonwhite people. Ordinary blacks and other nonwhite minorities are oppressed not only because of their poverty but also because of their racial or ethnic identities.

There is also no direct correlation between economic expansion or improved economic conditions and a decrease in racial inequality. In reality, racial discrimination often prevents African Americans and others from fully accessing the fruits of economic expansion.

After all, the black insurgency of the 1960s coincided with the robust and thriving economy of the 1960s — black people were rebelling because they were locked out of American affluence. Looking at racism as only a byproduct of economic inequality ignores the ways that racism exists as an independent force that wreaks havoc in the lives of all African Americans.

The <u>struggle against racism</u> regularly intersects with struggles for economic equality, but racism does not only express itself over economic questions. Antiracist struggles also take place in response to the social crises black communities experience, including struggles against racial profiling; police brutality; housing, health care, and educational inequality; and mass incarceration and other aspects of the "criminal justice" system.

> **Class struggle changes people's ideas and preconceptions and forges new bonds of solidarity. Working-class struggles have played a central role in winning white workers over to the fight against racism.**

Taking Racism Seriously
Jennifer Roesch • Jacobin • 8.8.2015

These fights against racial inequality are critical, both to improving the lives of African Americans and other racial and ethnic minorities in the here and now, and to demonstrating to ordinary white people the destructive impact of racism in the lives of nonwhite people.

Winning ordinary whites to an antiracist program is a key component in building a genuine, unified mass movement capable of challenging capital. Unity cannot be achieved by suggesting that black people should downplay the role of racism in our society so as not to alienate whites — while only focusing on the "more important" struggle against economic inequality.

This is why multiracial groupings of socialists have always participated in struggles against racism. This was particularly true throughout the twentieth century, as African Americans became a more urban population in constant conflict and competition with native-born and immigrant whites over jobs, housing, and schools. Violent conflict between working-class blacks and whites underlined the extent to which racial division destroyed the bonds of solidarity necessary to collectively challenge employers, landlords, and elected officials.

Socialists played key roles in campaigns against lynching and racism in the criminal justice system, like the Scottsboro Boys campaign in the 1930s, when nine African American youths were accused of raping

The struggle against racism regularly intersects with struggles for economic equality, but racism does not only express itself over economic concerns.

Winning ordinary whites to an antiracist program is a key component in building a genuine, unified mass movement.

two white women in Scottsboro, Alabama. The liberal National Association for the Advancement of Colored People (NAACP) had been reluctant to take the case, but the Scottsboro trials became a priority for the Communist Party and its affiliated International Legal Defense.

One part of the campaign involved touring the mothers of the boys around the country and then around the world to draw attention and support to their case. Ada Wright — mother to two of the boys — traveled to sixteen countries in six months in 1932 to tell her son's story. Because she was traveling with known Communists, she was often barred from speaking. In Czechoslovakia she was accused of being a Communist and jailed for three days before being expelled from the country.

Socialists were also involved in unionization drives among African Americans and were central to civil-rights campaigns in the North, South, and West for African Americans and other oppressed minorities. This engagement explains why many African Americans gravitated toward socialist politics over the course of their lives — socialists had always articulated a vision of society that could guarantee genuine black freedom.

The Black Belt Communists
Robin D.G. Kelley • Jacobin • 8.20.2015

24300

By the late 1960s, even figures like <u>Martin Luther King Jr</u> were describing a kind of socialist vision of the future. In a 1966 presentation to a gathering of his organization the Southern Christian Leadership Conference, King commented:

> We must honestly face the fact that the movement must address itself to the question of restructuring the whole of American society. There are forty million poor people here. And one day we must ask the question, "Why are there forty million poor people in America?" And when you begin to ask that question, you are raising questions about the economic system, about a broader distribution of wealth. When you ask that question, you begin to question the capitalistic economy …

> "Who owns the oil?" You begin to ask the question, "Who owns the iron ore?" You begin to ask the question, "Why is it that people have to pay water bills in a world that is two-thirds water?" These are questions that must be asked.

As movements continued to radicalize, groups like the Black Panthers and the League of Revolutionary Black Workers followed in the tradition of Malcolm X when they linked Black oppression directly to capitalism. The Panthers and the League went further than Malcolm by attempting to build socialist organizations for the specific purpose of organizing working-class blacks to fight for a socialist future.

Today the challenge for socialists is no different: being centrally involved in struggles against racism while also fighting for a world based on human need, not profit. ∎

We actually think that the struggle against racism is central to undoing the ruling class's power.

Aren't socialism and feminism sometimes in conflict?

Nicole Aschoff

Socialism and feminism have a long, and at times fraught, relationship.

Socialists are often accused of overemphasizing class — of placing the structural divide between those who must work for a wage to survive and those who own the means of production at the center of every analysis. Even worse they ignore or underplay how central other factors — like sexism, racism, or homophobia — are in shaping hierarchies of power. Or they admit the importance of these negative norms and practices, but argue that they can be rooted out only after we get rid of capitalism.

Meanwhile, socialists accuse mainstream feminists of focusing too much on individual rights rather than collective struggle and ignoring the structural divides between women. They accuse mainstream feminists of aligning themselves with <u>bourgeois political projects</u> that diminish the agency of working women or pushing middle-class demands that ignore the needs and desires

Hillary Clinton's Empowerment
Kevin Young & Diana C. Sierra Becerra • Jacobin • 3.9.2015

20512

of poor women, both in the global north and south.

These are old debates that date back to the mid-nineteenth century and the First International, and revolve around deeply political questions of power and the contradictions of capitalist society.

Muddying the waters further is how the politics of feminism is complicated by the historical nature of capitalism — the way sexism is integrated into both processes of profit making and the reproduction of the capitalist system as a whole is dynamic.

This dynamism is very apparent today when a female presidential candidate, Hillary Clinton, is the top choice among US millionaires. But the divide between socialism and feminism is ultimately an unnecessary one.

Why Socialists Should Be Feminists

The oppression of women, both in US society and globally, is multi-dimensional — gender divides in the political, economic, and social spheres underscore why, to free ourselves from the tyranny of capital, socialists must also be feminists.

The possibility of a woman finally becoming US president highlights the stark lack of female leadership, both in the US and around the world. Despite powerful women like Angela Merkel, Christine LeGarde, Janet Yellen, and Dilma Rousseff, the gender balance in politics and the corporate world remains highly skewed. Only 4 percent of CEOs at Fortune 500 firms are women and most corporate boards have few if any female members.

Globally, 90 percent of heads of state are men, and at the 2015 World Economic

Abortion Without Apology
Jenny Brown & Erin Mahoney • Jacobin • 12.31.2015

27772

Forum only 17 percent of the 2,500 representatives present were women, while 2013 marked the first time women held twenty seats in the US Senate.

Unlike many countries, women in the United States have, roughly speaking, equal rights and legal protection, as well as access to education, nutrition, and health care as men. But gender divides are apparent across society.

Women outperform men in higher education but they don't achieve comparable levels of success or wealth and remain stereotyped and under-represented in the popular media. Attacks on women's reproductive rights continue unabated and after a long, steady decline through the 1990s, rates of violence against women haven't budged since 2005.

At the same time, decisions about balancing home life and work life, in the face of ever-increasing housing and childcare costs, are as difficult as ever. In the fifty years since the passage of the 1963 Equal Pay Act women have entered the workforce en masse; today 60 percent of women work outside the home. Single and married mothers are even more likely to work, including 57 percent of mothers with children under the age of one.

Capital feeds on existing norms of sexism, compounding the exploitative nature of wage work.

But women who work full time still earn only 81 percent what men do — a number inflated by faster declines in men's wages (aside from the college educated) in recent years.

Pay gaps are matched by a gendered division of labor. The retail, service, and food sectors — the center of new job growth — are dominated by women, and the feminization of "care" work is even more pronounced. Despite recent gains, like the extension of the Fair Labor Standards Act to domestic workers, care work is still seen as women's work and undervalued. Disproportionate numbers of caring jobs are low-paying, contingent gigs in which humiliation, harassment, assault, and wage theft are common.

In addition to these clear differences between the experiences of men and women in the US there are more insidious, long-range effects of sexism. Feminists like bell hooks argue that sexism and racism pervade all corners of society and that dominant narratives of power glorify white, heteronormative visions of life.

From birth, boys and girls are treated differently and gender stereotypes introduced in the home, school, and everyday life are perpetuated throughout women's lives, shaping their identities and life choices.

Sexism also plays a less obvious, but critical, role in profit-making. From the beginning, capitalism has relied on unpaid labor outside the labor market (mainly in the home) that provides the essential ingredient for capital accumulation: workers — who must be created, clothed, fed, socialized, and loved.

This unpaid labor is highly gendered. While more men take part in household

Aren't socialism and feminism sometimes in conflict?

chores and child-rearing than in the past, social reproduction still falls primarily on women who are expected to shoulder the heaviest burden of household tasks. Most women also perform paid labor outside the

14168 Caring in the City
Johanna Brenner • Jacobin • Issue 15/16

" Even at their height, Nordic welfare states never came close to truly socializing the labor of care – especially when we think beyond child-rearing to the many kinds of care that people need over their lifetimes. "

home turning their work in the home into a "second shift." In this way, women are doubly oppressed — exploited in the workplace and unrecognized as workers in the social reproduction of labor.

Why Feminists Should Be Socialists

These persistent, cross-class gender divides — in the political, economic, and social spheres — fuel the dominant feminist viewpoint that sexism is a thing apart from capitalism, something that must be tackled separately.

Throughout numerous waves of feminist struggle, activists have pursued a variety of strategies for combating sexism and gender divides. Today, mainstream feminists gravitate toward a focus on putting women in power — both in the political and economic sphere — as a way to solve the range of problems women face, such as wage inequality, violence, work-life balance, and sexist socialization.

Prominent spokeswomen like Sheryl Sandberg, Hillary Clinton, Anne-Marie Slaughter, and many others advocate this "take-power" feminist strategy. Sandberg — one of the most influential proponents of this strategy — argues that women need to stop being afraid and start "disrupting the status quo." If they do, she believes this generation can close the leadership gap and in doing so make the world a better place for all women.

The thrust of the take-power argument is that if women were in power they, unlike men, would take care to implement policies that benefit women and that cross-class gender divides in economic, political, and cultural spheres will only be eliminated if

She Can't Sleep No More
Sarah Leonard • Jacobin • Issue 9

5602

women hold an equal number of leadership positions to men.

The emphasis on individual advancement as the path to achieving the goals of feminism is not new, and has been critiqued by numerous feminists including Charlotte Bunch and Susan Faludi who question the notion of sisterly solidarity as a remedy for deep-seated gender divides. As Faludi says, "You can't change the world for women by simply inserting female faces at the top of an unchanged system of social and economic power."

Socialist-feminists like Johanna Brenner also point to how mainstream feminism glosses over deep tensions among women:

> We can generously characterize as ambivalent the relationships between working-class women/poor women and the middle-class professional women whose jobs it is to uplift and regulate those who come to be defined as problematic — the poor, the unhealthy, the culturally unfit, the sexually deviant, the ill-educated. These class tensions bleed into feminist politics, as middle-class feminist advocates claim to represent working-class women.

So while it is certainly necessary to recognize how gendered contemporary society remains, it is also necessary to be clear-eyed about how to overcome these divides and, equally important, to recognize the limitations of a feminism that doesn't challenge capitalism.

Capital feeds on existing norms of sexism, compounding the exploitative nature of wage work. When women's ambitions and desires are silenced or under-valued, they are easier to take advantage of. Sexism is

To free ourselves from the tyranny of capital, socialists must also be feminists.

part of the company toolkit, enabling firms to pay women less — particularly women of color — and otherwise discriminate against them.

But even if we root out sexism, the inherent contradictions of capitalism will persist. It is important and necessary that women step into positions of power, but this won't change the fundamental divide between workers and owners — between women at the top and women at the bottom. It won't change the fact that most women find themselves in precarious, low-wage jobs that present a far greater barrier to advancement and a comfortable life than sexism in the economic or political sphere. It won't change the power of the profit motive and the compulsion of companies to give workers as little as economic, social, and cultural norms will allow.

Of course, society is not reducible to the wage relation and gender divides are real and persistent. Taking class seriously means anchoring the oppression of women within the material conditions in which they live and work while recognizing the role of sexism in shaping both women's work-life and their home life.

The feminist movement — both its "social-welfare" incarnation and its radical contemporary — has made significant gains. The challenge now is two-fold: to defend these hard-won victories and make it possible for all women to actually enjoy them, and to push forward with new, concrete demands that address the complex relationship between sexism and profit-making.

There is no simple answer to how to accomplish these twin goals. In the past, women have made the biggest gains by fighting for both women's rights and workers' rights simultaneously — linking the fight against sexism to the fight against capital.

As Eileen Boris and Anelise Orleck argue, during the 1970s and '80s "trade union feminists helped launch a revitalized women's movement that sparked new demands for women's rights at home, on the job, and within unions." Airline stewardesses, garment workers, clericals, and domestic workers challenged the male-dominated trade union movement (a woman didn't sit on the AFL-CIO executive board until 1980) and in the process forged a new, more expansive feminism.

Trade union women created a new field of possibility by demanding not only higher wages and equal opportunity but also childcare, flexible work schedules, pregnancy leave, and other gains usually overlooked or undervalued by their union brothers.

This is the direction that both socialists and feminists should be orienting themselves — toward struggles and demands that challenge both the drives of capital and the ingrained norms of sexism that are so deeply rooted under capitalism.

Struggles and demands that achieve this are concrete and are currently being fought for. For example, the struggle for single-payer health care — which would provide health care as a right to every person from cradle to grave regardless of their ability to pay — is a demand that undermines both sexism and the power of capital to control and repress worker agency. There are many other concrete short-term demands that blend the goals of feminism and socialism as well, including free higher education, free childcare, and a universal basic income combined with a robust social safety net.

These reforms would lay the groundwork for more radical goals that would go far in rooting out sexism, exploitation, and the commodification of social life. For example, projects to increase collective, democratic control over institutions central to our home, school, and work lives — schools, banks, workplaces, city governments, and state and local agencies — would give all women and men more power, autonomy, and the possibility for a better life.

This anticapitalist strategy is one that contains the possibility for the radical change that women need.

Ultimately the goals of radical feminism and socialism are the same — justice and equality for all people, not simply equal opportunity for women or equal participation by women in an unjust system. ■

Ultimately the goals of a radical feminism and socialism are the same — justice and equality for all people.

Wouldn't a more democratic world just mean a bigger environmental crisis?

Alyssa Battistoni

Capitalism is wreaking havoc on the world we live in. Climate change threatens to alter our planet beyond recognition, drowning coastal settlements, intensifying droughts and heat waves, and strengthening extreme weather.

The most harmful effects, of course, are falling on the world's poorest people. Overfishing has pushed fisheries to the point of collapse; fresh water supplies are scarce in regions that are home to half the world's population; fertilizer-intensive factory farming has exhausted agricultural land of nutrients; forests are being leveled at staggering rates to make way for cash crops and cattle ranches; extinction rates compare to those of prehistoric meteor-induced apocalypses.

These aren't issues that can be fixed by changing a lightbulb. Human activity has <u>transformed</u> the entire planet in ways that are now threatening the way we inhabit it — some of us far more than others. But if

The Anthropocene Myth
Andreas Malm • Jacobin • 3.30.2015

20875

We need to value the work of ecological production — to recognize that the activity of ecosystems keeps the earth viable for human life, and care for them accordingly.

you point out that it's not humanity in the abstract but capitalism that we should hold responsible, you'll hear a familiar retort: socialism is bad for the environment too! Production in the Soviet Union also ran on fossil fuels, degraded agricultural land, polluted rivers, and deforested vast expanses.

It's true that the USSR's environmental record doesn't inspire much confidence. But that doesn't mean that capitalism can solve our environmental problems, as bright-green entrepreneurs declare, or that modern industrial society must be abandoned altogether, as some deep greens would have it. Capitalism can certainly survive worsening environmental conditions, at least for a while — but it will survive under conditions of increasing eco-apartheid, with safety and comfort for the wealthy and growing scarcity for the rest.

Yet the twentieth-century socialist dream of maximizing production in the pursuit of abundance and equality seems increasingly untenable. Marxists held that communism would arise amid post-capitalist conditions of superabundance: once the capitalist engines were roaring, they could be seized and put to the benefit of all. But those engines can't run on fossil fuels any more, and contemporary consumer capitalism isn't the abundance we had in mind. We need not only to seize the means of production, but to transform them.

We also need a different vision of the future than has been put forth by the Left more recently. Environmental leftism of late has tended towards an anarchist bent that's distrustful of large-scale production and concentrated power, whether private or public. This shouldn't be surprising — because environmental problems are so place-specific, they often prompt small-scale local solutions. But climate change and other environmental crises arising from global systems of production and consumption are systemic issues of political economy; addressing them will require more than just pockets of alternative practice. And environmental problems don't respect political borders: ecological interdependence is another reminder that sustainability will come only through global solidarity.

To what future should twenty-first-century socialism aspire? How can we achieve a just society without relying on fossil fuels or exacerbating other forms of environmental destruction?

In figuring out an answer, socialists should look to socialist-feminist traditions concerned with the work that makes life livable. Socialist-feminists have long called attention to the labor of social reproduction — the activities necessary to replenish wage laborers both individually and across generations, such as education, childcare, housework, and food preparation. Struggles over social reproduction have focused on the demands and possibilities of life outside the factory, and they have much to teach us about organizing new ways of living. We also need to value the work of ecological reproduction — to recognize that the activity of ecosystems keeps the earth viable for human life, and care for them accordingly.

While some socialists aspire to a super-abundance of everything for everyone, environmentalists tend to point to over-consumption as a primary culprit of environmental degradation. But not all consumption is equivalent. Capitalism relies on cheap inputs in the form of labor and nature to make its cheap goods. As a result, the system consistently drives down both environmental and labor costs and standards. Inexpensive goods aren't necessarily bad, but they shouldn't come at the cost of working people and ecosystems. The goal of a socialist society is not to clamp down on popular consumption, but to create a society that emphasizes quality of life over quantity of things.

We need to find ways to live <u>luxuriously but also lightly</u>, aesthetically rather than ascetically. Instead of an endless cycle of working and shopping, life in a low-carbon socialist future would be oriented around activities that make life beautiful and fulfilling but require less intensive resource consumption: reading books, teaching, learning, making music, seeing shows, dancing, playing sports, going to the park, hiking, spending time with one another.

Robust provision of public goods makes it possible to enjoy communal luxuries while decreasing wasteful forms of private consumption. That means public housing that's affordable for all; free, extensive

Seize the Hamptons
Daniel Aldana Cohen • Jacobin • Issue 15/16

14170

The goal of a socialist society is not to clamp down on popular consumption, but to create a society that emphasizes quality of life over quantity of things.

transportation systems both within and between cities so that people can get around without owning a car; spacious parks and gardens that offer respite from daily life; support for arts and culture of a variety of forms; and plentiful spaces for public educational and recreational use, like libraries, basketball courts, and theaters. Cities are often touted as a key part of green futures on account of their energy-efficient density. But green cities require more than just urban planning and tall buildings. Socialism must reclaim the city as a space for struggle and solidarity in pursuit of needs and wants — to provide public resources as a means to emancipation and flourishing, and to insist on public places as spaces of beauty and pleasure.

Capitalists promise that technology will solve environmental problems. Technological solutions aren't a panacea, but we can't surrender technology to venture capitalists either: utopian socialist projects have long imagined a better world built from the combined abilities of humans, nature, and technology. And a host of current technologies, from clean energy sources to biotechnologies, promise to be part of a more sustainable future. But as long as they're privately controlled, produced only when profitable, and accessible only to those who can pay, their potential will be exploited only as it serves capitalists. A socialist society would support research into problems whose solutions aren't profitable and ensure that resulting technologies are put to use for public benefit.

Energy in particular is of central importance — energy use accounts for half of all carbon emissions and underpins modern life at every point. Renewable energy technologies, and solar power in particular, promise to be bountiful sources of clean energy. But while solar power is often touted as inherently small-scale and democratic, private companies are also assembling giant solar farms, positioning themselves as the conduit for a clean energy future. Meanwhile, deregulation and privatization of electric utilities in the neoliberal era has crippled the public's ability to build the new interconnected electric infrastructure that would make a major clean-energy transition possible. A socialist society could choose which energy sources to use and how quickly a transition should occur on the basis of knowledge about environmental and health benefits and social needs, rather than profit margins. We could produce clean energy on a large scale and build the infrastructure necessary to make it available to and affordable for all.

At the same time, new technologies don't in themselves constitute progress, tech companies' self-serving claims aside. New medical electronics, for example, don't always translate into better care; iPads don't translate into better education — in fact, the opposite is too often the case. A socialist society would make decisions about producing and implementing new technologies based on democratically chosen aims, rather than producing and consuming wastefully in order to keep various industries profitable. We could make sure everyone had access to clean, cheap electricity, for instance, before devoting resources to making electronic toys for the wealthy.

There will still be extractive activities, large-scale power plants, and industrial factories in a sustainable socialism. Some of these will be unsightly; some of them will disturb local ecosystems. But instead of dumping the harms of modern production on the people with the least power to resist them — such as workers, communities of color, and indigenous communities — we will make conscious decisions about what harms we'll accept and where and how they materialize, prioritizing the perspectives and needs of those who have long suffered from them. We could treat working landscapes as more than wastelands and recognize that the presence of machinery and industry doesn't have to mean devastation. We could pay the costs of minimizing environmental damage rather than cutting corners to beat the competition.

Capitalism began by enclosing public and common resources for private benefit and dispossessing their previous users. Collective ownership of the means of production should include common ownership of the land, oceans, and atmosphere. That would mean not only sharing in the resources that those spaces generate, but deciding together how they should be used. A socialist society could use scientific knowledge about ecological capacity to manage and regulate use of those spaces rather than ceding to industry whims: we'd listen to the 98 percent of scientists who say that anthropogenic climate change is happening, for example, rather than the lies of fossil-fuel lobbyists.

Under socialism, we would make decisions about resource use democratically, with regard to human needs and values rather than maximizing profit. An <u>ecologically sustainable socialism</u> isn't about preserving an idealized concept of pristine, untouched nature. It's about choosing the world we make and live in, and about recognizing that we share that world with species other than humans. A world that's livable is a world where everyone can have a good life instead of just scrambling to make a living.

That world will need forests as well as factories, wilderness refuges as well as cities. We'll seek to provide people with good work, but we'll also work less; we'll think about what work really needs to be done instead of creating jobs just to keep people employed. We'll choose to keep some spaces free of obvious human use, and to protect spaces for wildlife while also making it possible for people to escape city life to spend time in restored ecosystems. We'll aim to produce enough for everyone to live lives that are rich and full, rather than hoping for a long shot at accumulating private riches. With our needs provided for, we can realize our human potential in the context of leisurely social relationships to other humans and other species, with enough for everyone and time for what we will. ∎

9538

Alive in the Sunshine • Jacobin • Issue 13

Alyssa Battistoni • Jacobin • Issue 13

Under socialism, we would make decisions about resource use democratically, with regard to human needs and values rather than maximizing profit.

Are socialists pacifists? Aren't some wars justified?

Jonah Birch

In June 1918, Eugene Debs gave a speech that would land him in prison. Speaking in Canton, Ohio, the Socialist Party leader denounced President Woodrow Wilson and the Great War he had led the United States into.

For Debs, the mass slaughter that had raged across Europe for four bloody years was a conflict waged in the interests of capitalists, but fought by workers. In each country it was the rich who had declared war and stood to profit from it; but it was the poor who were sent to fight and die by the millions.

This, Debs told his audience, was how it had always been, as long as armies had been sent to battle one another in the name of king or country. "Wars throughout history have been waged for conquest and plunder," he said. "The master class has always declared the wars; the subject class has always fought the battles. The master class has had all to gain and nothing to lose, while the subject class has had nothing to gain and all to lose — especially their lives."

Debs's message to workers was a simple one: their enemy was not the people of Germany, the working-class soldiers they were being shipped off to murder; it was the rulers, on both sides, who ordered the troops into battle. It was the capitalists and their representatives in the American and German governments, whose wealth and power gave them control over the fates of millions.

Debs's speech was too much for authorities in the United States — they arrested him under a new law restricting free speech, the 1917 Espionage Act, and sentenced him to ten years in jail. Remarkably, in the 1920 election, Debs ran for president on the Socialist ticket while sitting in an Atlanta federal penitentiary, and still managed to win almost a million votes.

Making the World Safe for Capitalism

In the example of Debs, we can see the core ideas that have underpinned the socialist movement's approach to the question of war. Socialists have always seen capitalism's propensity for wars of conquest and plunder as the ultimate expression of the system's brutality. In the organization of state violence on an unprecedented scale, we see capitalism's tendency to subordinate human need to the logic of profit and power. In the gap between the promise of democratic equality and the reality of class oppression that war expresses, we see the fundamental injustice that defines our social order.

Under capitalism, exploitation occurs mostly through the market. It is the ostensibly non-coercive contractual relationship between workers and employers that masks deeper underlying class inequalities. But the war-making power of the capitalist state is still essential for the healthy functioning of the system. Capitalists in countries like the United States still rely on their own government's military, both to enforce the "rules of the game" in the global economy and to help them compete more effectively against other ruling classes.

Against this state of affairs, socialists support the organization of mass movements against the wars waged by our government. We participate in the struggle against restrictions on free speech and other democratic rights which inevitably accompany these wars. Against calls for "national unity," we fight for international solidarity and stronger class organization to fight for workers' interests. In the longer run, we aim to translate these movements into a broader struggle for a radical transformation of society along democratic lines.

Nowhere is this approach more important than in the United States — the most powerful capitalist country in the world. Today, the US spends more on its military than the next seven highest-spending countries combined. Our government has roughly eight hundred foreign military bases. American soldiers or allied troops are present in every region of the globe.

Over the past century and a half, the American state has waged brutal wars on behalf of a growing empire, from the 1898 Spanish-American War to the recent invasions of Afghanistan and Iraq. It has intervened again and again in Africa, Asia, and Latin America to protect the interests

Students Into Soldiers
Rory Fanning • Jacobin • 4.7.2016

30196

26507

Abolish the Military
Greg Shupak • Jacobin • 11.11.2015

of business and stamp out movements that might threaten its control over key resources or undermine the global capitalist system's stability.

Often these adventures were depicted as being necessary to bring freedom and democracy to oppressed countries, or to protect American citizens from danger. The historical record, however, tells a different story.

Even at the time of the 1898 Spanish-American War, considered by many to have been the dawn of modern American imperialism, the US government was invading Cuba, Puerto Rico, and the Philippines in the name of freeing their peoples from the yoke of Spanish colonialism. When, after victory was secured, Washington decided to make those three territories American protectorates (or in the case of Puerto Rico, an outright colony), it issued assurances that it had only the most benevolent intentions. And when the residents of those countries took these promises of freedom and democracy too literally, the United States decided it had no choice but to crush the popular independence struggles that emerged. In the Philippines, a nationalist insurrection that erupted in 1899 was put down at the cost of several hundred thousand Filipino lives.

In every war between then and now the pattern has been the same. The US government entered World War I in 1917 (after Wilson won the 1916 election on the basis of his antiwar pledges) to "make the world safe for democracy," while sending Marines all over Latin America in defense of capital's economic and political interests. It fought World War II to "free the world of tyranny," but spent the postwar years fixing elections in Italy, sponsoring a vicious civil war in Greece, and propping up the shah of Iran. It sent millions to their graves in Korea and Southeast Asia to "save" people there from Communism, while installing brutal dictatorships in both South Vietnam and South Korea. Meanwhile, US policy-makers covertly organized the overthrow of popular and democratic governments all over the globe — from Mohammad Mosaddegh in Iran to Patrice Lumumba in the Congo and Salvador Allende in Chile.

To justify these campaigns, American officials have often resorted to vicious racism. General William Westmoreland once justified the brutality of the forces he led in Vietnam by saying that "The Oriental doesn't put the same high price on life as does a Westerner ... We value life and human dignity. They don't care about life and human dignity."

At every turn, the American government has <u>shown</u> its commitment to democracy and freedom abroad to be as shallow as its commitment to equality at home. Again and again, it has proven that its fear of democratic control over the world's resources ran deeper than its pro-democratic rhetoric. As Henry Kissinger, who served as a foreign-policy advisor to three presidents, said of the efforts by the Nixon administration to topple Chile's elected socialist government, "I don't see why we need to stand by and watch a country go communist because of the irresponsibility of its own people." The same went for 1980s attempts to undermine leftist governments in tiny Nicaragua and even tinier Grenada.

More recently, this pattern has been repeated in the Middle East — now the central battleground for the US and its

Nixon and the Cambodian Genocide
Brett S. Morris • Jacobin • 4.27.2015

21447

imperial competitors, because of its role as the center of global oil production.

If the wars in Iraq and Afghanistan were initially justified as necessary to defend American lives, destroy Al Qaeda, and eradicate terrorism, they accomplished none of those aims. Nor have they resulted in democratic governments in either country. On the contrary, the hundreds of thousands of lives lost in these wars have only destabilized the region and intensified sectarian divisions. Rather than supporting democratic movements, the United States has backed dictatorial regimes in Egypt and Bahrain, and helped strengthen the most vicious and reactionary monarchies in Saudi Arabia and the United Arab Emirates.

The United States has also allowed Israel to escalate its daily violence (with semi-regular bouts of mass killings in Gaza), occupation, and settlement expansion at the expense of Palestinians. And it has watched as the contending sides in the Syrian civil war have overseen a slaughter that has drowned the Syrian struggle for democracy in the blood of hundreds of thousands of citizens.

Given the scope and scale of American imperial violence, it's crucial that socialists in the United States oppose their government's military interventions. Such a stance is necessary for any genuine working-class solidarity. Every time the US government blows up an Afghan wedding party or helps protect a death squad in Iraq; every time it sends someone to rot in a prison in Afghanistan or Guantanamo Bay; every time it allows the CIA to torture a prisoner; it makes class solidarity across borders less likely.

Why should workers in other countries ally themselves with those in the United

States, in whose name they are bombed and occupied? To the extent that Americans buy into the nationalism that inevitably goes along with their government's machinations abroad, they make the emergence of a class-based movement against oppression and exploitation impossible.

Meanwhile, the position of American workers only deteriorates further. When hundreds of billions of dollars are spent attacking countries around the globe, it isn't available for social welfare programs that could help those at home. The waste of blood and resources, the racism, and the reactionary upsurges that are the handmaidens of wars abroad all rebound to the detriment of workers in the US. At a time when millions of Americans are suffering from unemployment and poverty, the more than $2 trillion spent on the invasion and occupation of Iraq seems increasingly obscene.

All this means that the American labor movement has a material incentive to oppose its own government's drive to war. It is for this reason that socialists think an international working-class movement against war and imperialism is not only necessary, but also possible.

The Enemy at Home

However, if socialists in a country like the United States are opposed to the wars fought by their governments, that does not mean they are pacifists — that is, that they oppose all wars or have a principled stance against any kind of violence. The question is who is waging the war and on behalf of what interests or policies.

As the nineteenth-century military theorist Carl von Clausewitz noted, "War is a continuation of politics by other means." Clausewitz meant that to understand the character of a given war, you had to understand who was fighting it and for what purpose. Of course, Clausewitz, a Prussian general in the Napoleonic Wars, was hardly a left-wing radical, but his basic point is an important one for socialists to understand.

The socialist movement wants to eradicate war because it is brutal and irrational — a waste of human life and social resources that produces enormous devastation. But in a world filled with exploitation and oppression, one has to differentiate between the violence of those fighting to maintain injustice, and those fighting against injustice.

One cannot, for example, conflate the violence of South African apartheid with that of the armed elements of Nelson Mandela's African National Congress. The same goes for the violence of the American military during the Vietnam War — a war that eventually killed as many as 3.5 million people — and that of the Vietnamese National Liberation Front, which fought to free Vietnam from French and American domination.

For the socialist movement, Clausewitz's dictum points to the need to assess any war on the basis of the interests it serves. It's no coincidence that socialists like Marx and Engels supported the Union in the Civil War, recognizing that despite Lincoln's stated intention to reunite the country without doing away with slavery, a <u>war</u> against the Confederacy would necessarily become a war against the planter class. In fact, as Lincoln — who in the 1840s opposed

Are socialists pacifists? Aren't some wars justified?

the Mexican-American War because he saw it as an effort to expand slavery to new territories — came to recognize, the North could only succeed by mobilizing slaves in a battle for their own freedom.

> A conservative estimate of civilian deaths arising from the war is two million in South Vietnam alone, from a population of nineteen million. An analogous civilian casualty rate in the United States today would be nearly thirty-three million."

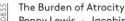

10835 The Burden of Atrocity
Penny Lewis • Jacobin • 4.29.2014

None of this is to suggest that socialists have a purely instrumental approach to violence — that we think, as is so often claimed, that "the ends justify of the means." In our efforts to achieve the kind of change we seek, violence can only undermine our cause over the long term; we can never hope to match the capacity for violence of the capitalist state, and our movement will only be weakened insofar as the struggle for socialism is transformed from a social and political conflict into a military one.

Nor are we necessarily supportive of governments just because they happen to be in conflict with our own: we do not excuse the imperial violence of, for instance, Russia and China simply because they are occasionally at loggerheads with our own rulers.

More fundamentally, it is important to be clear that our support for groups fighting against their oppression, at the hands of the US government or anyone else, does not mean that we're always uncritical of these forces. One need only look at the growing levels of inequality and the increasing penetration of global capitalism in South Africa since the fall of apartheid, or in Vietnam since its liberation, to see that even victorious struggles need not produce a truly just outcome. Indeed, while expressing solidarity with movements challenging oppression, socialists must be willing to criticize those waging these struggles, whenever necessary — whether that criticism is made on political, strategic, or even moral grounds.

But neither do we treat all sides in a particular conflict as if they were the same. Above all, we oppose our own government's role in propagating wars, or expanding its military and political influence, at the expense of the working classes of the world. As the German revolutionary Karl Liebknecht put it in a speech during World War I, we understand that "the main enemy is at home."

On that basis, we hope to forge an internationalist movement that can not only challenge a particular imperial intervention, but can come to pose a threat to the very foundations of a system that breeds war and mass violence on a scale unprecedented in history.

Beyond Imperialism

Today, the Left is far too weak to accomplish that goal. In the United States, the labor movement lacks the capacity for sustained activity against war. But what the example of Eugene Debs shows us is that there is a long history of radical opposition to imperialism from which we can draw hope and inspiration.

That tradition of left-wing anti-imperialism lived on after Debs himself died. If it lost steam during the Cold War years of McCarthyite repression after World War II, it was revived during the 1960s and 1970s. Figures such as Martin Luther King Jr became increasingly vocal critics of the Vietnam War. Although he is often depicted as an anodyne moralist, a precursor to multicultural liberalism, King was actually a visionary whose politics became increasing radical in tandem with the movement he led. Nothing expressed that growing radicalism better than his decision to publicly oppose the Vietnam War — a move which even his closest advisors recommended against because of its potential political consequences.

Vietnam: The (Last) War the U.S. Lost
Joe Allen • Haymarket Books • 2007

Ignoring their counsel, on April 4, 1967, exactly one year before his assassination, King delivered the most controversial speech of his career. Speaking at New York's Riverside Church, he came out against the Vietnam War and called on the Johnson administration to halt its unprecedented bombing campaign and initiate a withdrawal of the half-million US troops in Southeast Asia.

Decrying the "madness" of the Democratic administration's policy, King focused on the incredible brutality that ordinary people in Vietnam faced at the hands of the American military. "They must see Americans as strange liberators," he concluded, when that supposed liberation involved propping up corrupt, undemocratic governments, destroying entire villages, defoliating the countryside with napalm and Agent Orange, and killing women, children, and the elderly.

And what of the US soldiers, overwhelmingly working-class kids drawn from poverty-stricken rural communities and segregated urban ghettoes? Noting the disproportionate number of African Americans who had been sent to kill and die in the swamps of Vietnam, King castigated the administration for "taking the black young men who had been crippled by our society and sending them eight thousand miles away to guarantee liberties in Southeast Asia which they had not found in southwest Georgia and East Harlem."

King pointed out that the hopes for a real effort to combat poverty in the US that had been inspired by Johnson's Great Society program had been destroyed by the escalation in Vietnam. A genuine campaign to eradicate poverty at home was impossible,

In a world filled with exploitation and oppression, one has to differentiate between the violence of those fighting to maintain injustice, and those fighting against injustice.

he had concluded, "so long as adventures like Vietnam continued to draw men and skills and money like some demonic, destructive suction tube."

Given all this, King said that he could no longer keep silent, despite the strong pressure from his supposed allies in the Johnson administration to avoid public criticism of the government's Vietnam policy. Comparing the incredible scale of the violence in Vietnam to the relatively minor destruction produced by a series of riots that had broken out in many of America's big cities — which had caused much hand-wringing in the press over the threat posed by "black extremists" — King described his realization "that I could never again raise my voice against the violence of the oppressed in the ghettos without having first spoken clearly to the greatest purveyor of violence in the world today: my own government." A few days later, he marched in a mass protest against the war in New York's Central Park.

King's speech, known to posterity as "Beyond Vietnam," earned him the ire of even previously sympathetic figures in the liberal establishment. He was disinvited from a planned visit with Johnson at the White House. One of the president's advisors wrote privately that King had "thrown in his lot with the commies." Meanwhile, he was attacked in editorials that appeared the next day in 168 major newspapers. The New York Times wrote that his denunciation of the war was "wasteful and self-defeating." The Washington Post did them one better, saying of King, "he has diminished his usefulness to his cause, his country, and his people."

What King came to <u>understand</u> was that racism and inequality at home, and war abroad, were interlinked. This recognition put him at odds with his erstwhile liberal supporters, whose willingness to challenge the status quo ended — as it so often has for the liberal establishment — when America's position as the world's strongest imperial power came into question.

Yet in confronting these questions, and challenging his former friends, King was taking on a set of issues any mass social movement that makes serious advances in the United States will eventually have to face: one can't talk about social change at home while ignoring the carnage generated by American foreign policy. For the US left, and especially any future socialist movement here, that's a lesson worth learning. ∎

Socialists want to eradicate war because it is brutal and irrational. But we think there's a difference between the violence of the oppressed and that of the oppressors.

Why do socialists talk so much about workers?

Vivek Chibber

Most people know that socialists place the working class at the center of their political vision. But why exactly? When I put this question to students or even to activists, I get a range of answers, but the most common response is a moral one — socialists think that workers suffer the most under capitalism, making their plight the most important issue to focus on.

Now it is true, of course, that workers face all sorts of indignities and material deprivation, and any movement for social justice has to take this as a central issue. But if this is all there is to it, if this is the only reason we should focus on class, the argument falls apart pretty easily. After all, there are lots of groups who suffer indignities and injustices — racial minorities, women, the disabled. Why single out workers? Why not just say that every marginal and oppressed group ought to be at the heart of socialist strategy?

Yet there is more to the focus on class than just the moral argument. The reason socialists believe that class organizing has to be at the center of a <u>viable political strategy</u> also has to do with two other practical factors: a diagnosis of what the sources of injustice are in modern society, and a prognosis of what are the best levers for change in a more progressive direction.

Capitalism Won't Deliver

There are many things that people need to lead decent lives. But two items are absolutely essential. The first is some guarantee of material security — things like having an income, housing, and basic health care. The second is being free of social domination — if you are under someone else's control, if they make many of the key decisions for you, then you are constantly vulnerable to abuse. So, in a society in which most people don't have job security, or have jobs but can't pay their bills, in which they have to submit to other people's control, in which they don't have a voice in how laws and regulations are made — it's impossible to achieve social justice.

Capitalism is an economic system that depends on depriving the vast majority of people of these essential preconditions for a decent life. Workers show up for work every day knowing that they have little job security; they are paid what employers feel is consistent with their main priority, which is making profits, not the well-being of employees; they work at a pace and duration that is set by their bosses; and they submit to these conditions, not because they want to, but because for most of them, the alternative to accepting these conditions is not having a job at all. This is not some incidental or marginal aspect

19550

Labor Law Won't Save Us
Joe Burns • Jacobin • 1.27.2015

> The labor movement is not just another social movement. It has a special role: to challenge the main source of power in society — accumulation of capital from the labor of workers.

of capitalism. It is the defining feature of the system.

Economic and political power is in the hands of capitalists, whose only goal is to maximize profits, which means that the condition of workers is, at best, a secondary concern to them. And that means that the system is, at its very core, unjust.

Holding the Lever

It follows that the first step to making our society more humane and fair is to reduce the insecurity and material deprivation in

Workers are not only a social group that is systematically exploited, they are also the group best positioned to enact real change.

so many people's lives, and to increase their scope for self-determination. But we immediately run into a problem — the political resistance of elites.

Power is not distributed equally in capitalism. Capitalists decide who is hired and fired, and who works for how long, not workers. Capitalists also have the most political power, because they can do things like lobby, fund political campaigns, and bankroll political parties. And since they are the ones who benefit from the system, why should they encourage changes in it, changes that inevitably mean a diminution in their power and their bottom line? The answer is, they don't take very kindly to challenges, and they do their best to maintain the status quo.

Movements for progressive reform have found time and again that whenever they try to push for changes in the direction of justice, they come up against the power of capital. Any reforms that require a redistribution of income, or come from the government as a social measure — whether it's health care, environmental regulations, minimum wages, or job programs — are routinely opposed by the wealthy, because any such measures inevitably mean a reduction in their income (as taxes) or their profits. What this means is that progressive reform efforts have to find a source of leverage, a source of power that will enable them to overcome the resistance of the capitalist class and its political functionaries.

The working class has this power, for a simple reason — capitalists can only make their profits if workers show up to work every day, and if they refuse to play along, the profits dry up overnight. And if there is one thing that catches employers' attention, it's when the money stops flowing.

Actions like strikes don't just have the potential to bring particular capitalists to their knees, they can have an impact far beyond, on layer after layer of other institutions that directly or indirectly depend on them — including the government. This ability to crash the entire system, just by refusing to work, gives workers a kind of leverage that no other group in society has, except capitalists themselves. This is why, if progressive social change requires overcoming capitalist opposition — and we have learned over three centuries that it does — then it is of central importance to organize workers so that they can use that power.

Workers are therefore not only a social group that is systematically oppressed and exploited in modern society, they are also the group that is best positioned to enact real change and extract concessions from the major center of power — the bankers and industrialists who run the system. They are the group that comes into contact with capitalists every day and are tied in a perennial conflict with them as a part of their very existence. They are the only group that has to take on capital if they want to improve their lives. There is no more logical force to organize a political movement around.

Why Class Matters
Erik Olin Wright • Jacobin • 12.23.2015

26897

And this isn't just a theory. If we look back at the conditions in which far-reaching reforms have been passed over the past hundred years, reforms which improved the material conditions of the poor, or which gave them more rights against the market — they were invariably based on working-class mobilization. This is true not only with the "color-blind" measures of the welfare state, but even with such phenomena as civil rights and the struggle for the vote.

Any movement that extended benefits to the poor, whether they were black or white, male or female, had to base itself on a mobilization of working people. This was true in Europe and the Global South as much as it was in the United States.

It is this power to extract real concessions from capital that makes the working class so important for political strategy. Of course, the fact that workers also form the majority in every capitalist society and that they are systematically exploited only makes their plight all the more pressing. This combination of moral urgency and strategic force is why socialist politics is based on the working class. ∎

Workers are at the heart of the capitalist system. And that's why they are at the center of socialist politics.

*Will socialism
be boring?*

Danny Katch

The year was 2081, and everybody was finally equal. They weren't only equal before God and the law. They were equal every which way. Nobody was smarter than anybody else. Nobody was better looking than anybody else. Nobody was stronger or quicker than anybody else. All this equality was due to the 211th, 212th, and 213th Amendments to the Constitution, and to the unceasing vigilance of agents of the United States Handicapper General.

This is not my version of 2081, but Kurt Vonnegut's in the opening lines of his "Harrison Bergeron," a short story about a future in which everyone is the same. Attractive people are forced to wear masks, smart people have earpieces that regularly distract their thoughts with loud noises, and so on.

As one would expect with Vonnegut, there are some darkly hilarious moments — such as a ballet performance in which the dancers are shackled with leg weights — but unlike most of his stories, "Harrison Bergeron" is based on a reactionary premise: equality can only be achieved by reducing the most talented down to the mediocre ranks of the masses.

Socialism has often been portrayed in science fiction in these types of gray dystopian terms, which reflect the ambivalence that many artists have toward capitalism. Artists are often repulsed by the anti-human values and commercialized culture of their society, but they are also aware that they have a unique status within it that allows them to express their creative individuality — <u>as long as it sells</u>. They fear that socialism would strip them of that status and reduce them to the level of mere workers, because they are unable to imagine a world that values and encourages the artistic expression of all of its members.

Of course there's another reason that socialist societies are imagined to be grim and dreary: most of the societies that have called themselves socialist have been grim and dreary. Shortly after the revolutions in Eastern Europe that ended the domination of the Soviet Union, the Rolling Stones played a legendary concert in Prague in which they were welcomed as cultural heroes.

The catch is that this was 1990, Mick and Keith were almost fifty, and it had been years since their most recent hit, a song called "Harlem Shuffle" that is god-awful. Forget about the censored books and the bans on demonstrations. If you want to understand how boring Stalinist society was, watch the video for "Harlem Shuffle" and then think about one of the coolest cities in Europe going out of its mind with joy at the chance to see those guys.

Culture Isn't Free
Miranda Campbell • Jacobin • 7.2.2015

23040

To be an effective socialist, it is extremely helpful to like human beings.

Does it really matter if socialism is boring? Perhaps it seems silly, even offensive, to be concerned about such a trivial matter compared to the horrors that capitalism inflicts all the time. Think about the dangers of increasing hurricanes and wildfires caused by climate change, the trauma of losing your home or your job, or the insecurity of not knowing if the man sitting next to you sees you as a target for date rape. We like watching movies about the end of the world or people facing adversity, but in our actual lives most of us prefer predictability and routine.

Worrying that socialism might be boring can seem like the ultimate "white people problem," as the Internet likes to say. Sure it would be nice to eliminate poverty, war, and racism ... but what if I get bored?

But it does matter, of course, because we don't want to live in a society without creativity and excitement, and also because if those things are being stifled then there must be a certain ruling clique or class that is doing the stifling — whether or not they think it's for our own good. Finally, if socialism is stale and static, it will never be able to replace capitalism, which can accurately be called many nasty things, but boring is not one of them.

Capitalism has revolutionized the world many times over in the past two hundred years and changed how we think, look, communicate, and work. Just in the past few decades, this system adapted quickly and effectively to the global wave of protests and strikes in the sixties and seventies: unionized factories were closed and relocated to other corners of the world, the stated role of government was shifted from helping people to helping corporations help people, and finally all these changes and others as well were sold to us as what the protesters had been fighting for all along — a world in which every man, woman, and child is born with the equal right to buy as many smartphones and factory-ripped jeans as they want.

Capitalism can reinvent itself far more quickly than any previous economic order. "Conservation of the old modes of production in unaltered form," write Marx and Engels in *The Communist Manifesto*, is "the first condition of existence for all earlier industrial classes. Constant revolutionizing of production, uninterrupted disturbance of all social conditions, everlasting uncertainty and agitation distinguish the capitalist epoch from all earlier ones." While earlier class societies desperately tried to maintain the status quo, capitalism thrives on overturning it.

The result is a world in constant motion. Yesterday's factory district is today's slum is tomorrow's hipster neighborhood. All that is solid melts into air. That's another line from the *Manifesto* and also the name of a <u>wonderful book</u> by Marshall Berman, who writes that to live in modern capitalism is "to find ourselves in an environment that promises us adventure, power, joy,

All That Is Solid Melts Into Air: The Experience of Modernity
Marshall Berman • Verso Books • 1983

growth, transformation of ourselves and the world — and at the same time, that threatens to destroy everything we have, everything we know, everything we are."

Yet most of our lives are far from exciting. We work for bosses who want us to be mindless drones. Even when a cool, new invention comes to our workplace, we can count on it to eventually be used to make us do more work in less time, which might arouse the passions of management, but will only fill our days with more drudgery.

Outside of work, it's the same story. Schools see their primary role as providing "career readiness," which is an inoffensive phrase that means getting kids prepared to handle the bullshit of work. Even the few hours that are supposed to be our own are mostly spent on laundry, cooking, cleaning, checking homework, and all the other necessary tasks to get ourselves and our families ready for work the next day.

Most of us only experience the excitement of capitalism as something happening somewhere else: new gadgets for rich people, wild parties for celebrities, amazing performances to watch from your couch. On the bright side, at least most of it is better than "Harlem Shuffle."

Even worse, when we do get to directly touch the excitement, it's usually because we're on the business end of it. It's our jobs being replaced by that incredible new robot, our rent becoming too expensive ever since the beautiful luxury tower was built across the street. Adding insult to injury, we are then told if we complain that we are standing in the way of progress.

The sacrifice of individuals in the name of societal progress is said to be one of

24680

The Privatization of Childhood
Megan Erickson • Jacobin • 9.3.2015

the horrors of socialism, a world run by faceless bureaucrats supposedly acting for the common good. But there are plenty of invisible and unelected decision-makers under capitalism, from health insurance officials who don't know us but can determine whether our surgery is "necessary" to billionaire-funded foundations that declare schools they have never visited to be "failures."

Socialism also involves plenty of change, upheaval, and even chaos, but this chaos, as Hal Draper might have said, <u>comes from below</u>. During the Russian Revolution, the Bolshevik-led Soviet government removed marriage from the control of the church one month after taking power and allowed couples to get divorced at the request of either partner.

These laws dramatically changed family dynamics and women's lives, as evidenced by some of the song lyrics that become popular in rural Russian villages:

> Time was when my husband used his fists and force. But now he is so tender. For he fears divorce. I no longer fear my husband. If we can't cooperate, I will take myself to court, and we will separate.

Of course, divorce can be heartbreaking as well as liberating. Revolutions cast everything in a new light, from our leaders to our loved ones, which can be both exciting and excruciating. "Gigantic events," wrote Trotsky in a 1923 newspaper article, "have descended on the family in its old shape, the war and the revolution. And following them came creeping slowly the underground mole — critical thought, the conscious study and evaluation of family relations and forms of life. No wonder that this process reacts in the most intimate and hence most painful way on family relationships."

In another article, Trotsky described daily experience in revolutionary Russia as "the process by which everyday life for the working masses is being broken up and formed anew." Like capitalism, these first steps toward socialism offered both the promise of creation and the threat of destruction, but with the crucial difference that the people Trotsky wrote about were playing an active role in determining how their world was changing.

They were far from having complete control, especially over the mass poverty and illiteracy that the tsar and world war had bequeathed to them. But even in these miserable conditions, the years between the October Revolution and Stalin's final consolidation of power demonstrated the excitement of a society in which new doors are open to the majority classes for the first time.

There was an explosion of art and culture. Cutting-edge painters and sculptors decorated the public squares of Russian cities with their futurist art. For the record, Lenin hated the futurists, but this didn't stop the government from funding their journal, *Art of the Commune*. Ballets and theaters were opened up to mass audiences. Cultural groups and workers' committees came together to bring art and artistic training into factories. The filmmaker Sergei Eisenstein gained world renown for the groundbreaking technique of his movies depicting the Russian Revolution.

The silly premise of "Harrison Bergeron" was refuted. Socialism didn't find talented artists to be a threat to "equality" or find a contradiction between appreciating individual artists and opening up the previously elitist art world to the masses of workers and peasants.

The possibilities of socialism that the world glimpsed in Russia for a few years were not a sterile experiment controlled by a handful of theorists but a messy and thrilling creation of tens of millions of people groping toward a different way of running society and treating one another, with all the skills, impediments, and neuroses they had acquired through living under capitalism, in the horrible circumstances of a poor, war-torn country. They screwed up in all sorts of ways, but they also showed that socialism is a real possibility, not a utopian dream that doesn't fit the needs of real human beings.

And the society they were pointing toward was a place where equality meant not lowering but raising the overall cultural and intellectual level of society. In the many novels, movies, and other artistic renderings of socialism, there is little mention of rising divorce rates and heated debates about art. Most of them imagine societies without conflict, which is why they seem so creepy — including the ones intending to promote socialism.

A similar problem exists inside many protest movements today, in which some activists want to organize movements and meetings around a consensus model, which means that almost everybody present has to agree on a decision for it to get passed. Consensus can sometimes be an effective way to build trust among people who don't know and trust one another, especially because most people in this supposedly

Most of us only experience the excitement of capitalism as something happening somewhere else: new gadgets for rich people, wild parties for celebrities, amazing performances to watch from your couch.

democratic society have almost no experience participating in the democratic process of discussion, debate, and then a majority-rule vote.

When organizers view consensus not only as a temporary tactic but as a model for how society should be run, however, there is a problem. I want to live in a democratic society with conflicts and arguments, where people aren't afraid to stand up for what they believe in and don't feel pressured to soften their opinions so that, when a compromise is reached, we can pretend that we all agreed in the first place. If your case for socialism rests on the idea that people will stop getting into arguments and even occasionally acting like jerks, you should probably find another cause.

Socialism isn't going to be created, Lenin once wrote, with "abstract human material, or with human material specially prepared by us, but with the human material bequeathed to us by capitalism. True, that is no easy matter, but no other approach to this task is serious enough to warrant discussion."

To be an effective socialist, it is extremely helpful to like human beings. Not humanity as a concept but real, sweaty people. In *All That Is Solid Melts into Air*, Berman tells a story about Robert Moses, the famous New York City public planner who flattened entire neighborhoods that stood in the way of the exact spots where he envisioned new highways. Moses, a friend once said, "loved the public, but not as people." He built parks, beaches, and highways for the masses to use, even as he loathed most of the working-class New Yorkers he encountered.

Loving the public but not people is also a feature of elitist socialists, whose faith rests more on five-year development plans, utopian blueprints, or winning future elections than on the wonders that hundreds of millions can achieve when they are inspired and liberated. That is why their visions for socialism are so lifeless and unimaginative.

By contrast, Marx, who is often presented as an isolated intellectual, was a rowdy, argumentative, funny, passionate person who once declared that his favorite saying was the maxim: "I am a human being, I consider nothing that is human alien to me." I find it hard to see how a world run by the majority of human beings, with all of our gloriously and infuriatingly different talents, personalities, madnesses, and passions, could possibly be boring. ∎

Socialism isn't about inducing bland mediocrity. It's about unleashing the creative potential of all.

Notes

Notes

Notes

Notes